MW00764681

LEXICAL SEMANTICS

Extraordinary Words for
Extraordinary People

Other Books by This Author

Take Counsel, Universal Publishers, Parkland, Florida, 2000.

North Carolina Automobile Insurance Law, The Harrison Company Publishers, Norcross, Georgia, First Edition, 1988.

A Lawyer Prays God's Will for His Clients, Universal Publishers, Boca Raton, Florida, 2000.

North Carolina Corporation Law and Practice Forms, West Group, St. Paul, Minnesota, Fourth Edition, 2003.

The Saga of Joe Monk, "The Greatest Golfer of Olive Chapel", Universal Publishers, Boca Raton, Florida 2000.

North Carolina Corporation Law and Practice, West Group, St. Paul Minnesota, Fourth Edition, 2003.

The Conservative Mind " A New Model for Government". Universal Publishers, Boca Raton, Florida, 2004.

Snyder North Carolina Corporation Law and Practice Forms, The Harrison Company Publishers, Norcross, Georgia, First Edition,1990.

Snyder North Carolina Corporation Law and Practice, The Harrison Company Publishers, Norcross, Georgia, First Edition, 1992.

North Carolina Automobile Insurance Law, The Harrison Company Publishers, Norcross, Georgia, Second Edition, 1994.

Snyder North Carolina Corporation Law and Practice Forms, The Harrison Company Publishers, Norcross, Georgia Second Edition, 1995.

Snyder North Carolina Corporation Law and Practice, The Harrison Company Publishers, Norcross, Georgia, Second Edition, 1995.

North Carolina Automobile Insurance Law, The Harrison Company Publishers, Suwanee, Georgia, Third Edition, 1999.

Snyder North Carolina Corporation Law and Practice Forms, The Harrison Company Publishers, Suwanee, Third Edition, 1999.

Snyder North Carolina Corporation Law and Practice, The Harrison Company Publishers, Suwanee, Georgia, Third Edition, 1999.

LEXICAL SEMANTICS

Extraordinary Words for
Extraordinary People

*(Magnificently Complex and
Unknown to Most Scholars)*

Now Yours Via
The One Word Definition

James E. Snyder, Jr., J.D.

LEXICAL SEMANTICS
Extraordinary Words for
Extraordinary People

Copyright 2007 James E. Snyder, Jr., J.D.
All rights reserved.

BrownWalker Press
Boca Raton, Florida
USA 2007
www.BrownWalker.com

Hardcover
ISBN: 1-59942-418-5
ISBN-13: 978-1-59942-418-7

Ebook
ISBN: 1-59942-419-3
ISBN-13: 978-1-59942-419-4

Publisher: Jeff Young
Acquisitions Editor: Rebekah Galy
Cover Design: Shereen Siddiqui
Interior Layout: Mianna Vaccaro

DEDICATION

To my sister

Jean Olive

A graceful lady who
most taught me to aspire

Acknowledgments

Those of us who read and write extensively, as the years flash by, inexorably become enamored with our mother language. From Latin and Greek to the words of the Anglo-Saxons and as spiced through the centuries with French, Spanish, German and now African, Southeast Asian and Southern Asian condiments, the English language, as was Latin historically, is the international language. John Adams presaged this evolution.

Our respective utilities of this poetic and euphonious means of communication are as varied as the tens of thousands of words with which we attempt to communicate. My first recollection is that of my mother carefully printing, before my young eyes, my name. Unfortunately, through the decades of formal education, the study of the English language for me became a labor. Love was neither lost nor found – until recently. Happily, this great language currently is a most fond companion.

I am indebted eternally to the many great teachers, instructors and professors who inculcated in my small mind, usually per force, the basis for my own conclusion, to wit: "After all that education, I knew the basics and not much more". As expressed in the preface of this volume, I was aware that I both lacked the force of mind to be able to unlock in some simple fashion those remaining beautiful and complex words used only by the truly great writers.

Competition can be a means for epiphanal thinking. So for me the rendition of the log jam of my thinking had been foreordained during nascent years by my parents who provided an opportunity for equal hours of play, study and athletics. The many fine coaches in my life, among others, Coaches Coy Temple, Jim Mashburn, Frank King, Bob Calicutt, V.G. Price and Pres Mull through secondary school; Coaches Bones McKinney, Dean Smith, Jack Murdock, Jim Layton and Jack McClosky through university years; and, my association as unpaid high school assistant with Coaches Richard Jones and Mike Gurley, all contributed. Athletics, after all, is a matter of replicating the older and better players and the discovery of geodesic paths to the basket or goal line with a slight fake and explosion toward the target.

Accordingly, this acknowledgement spans my lifetime and creates debts never to be repaid. Because of the combinations of educational and athletic experiences, it became apparent that most of us remain resistant to the spectacular words of our language without a key to unlock the safe within which they reside. By means of one word definitions, it is my sincere hope that some might feel a small portion of the debt of gratitude to your own teachers, professors and coaches and even to mine.

The last thing my family wanted me to do was to write another book. Once more they and now even our grandchildren, from whose attention these projects take me, are understanding.

My faithful staff, including Cindy Venable, Iris Hyatt, Chasity Clodfelter, Jennifer Wagoner, Kristina Homesley, and Elizabeth Lancaster once more have abided idiosyncrasies and performed the extra tasks required to permit the completion of this book.

I express particular gratitude to two of my assistants to whom this book was primarily assigned. Abby Younts and Erin Younts have worked tirelessly and with remarkable precision in transcribing, proofing and assisting me in coordinating the final work which is before us. For these reasons and for abiding the exasperation of coordinating and living with a mundane book about words, I express to them my thanks.

Finally, the only acknowledgement which I seek is an awareness that this effort might have enabled a number of interested persons to crack that cold, hard, steely, and seemingly impenetrable safe which heretofore has been the "sangfroid" harbinger and cache of a magnificent wealth of words.

♒ *JES*

Table of Contents

Table of Contents Continued

Book II

Preface

I had returned from a trip to Germany and was determined to learn the language of my forefathers. But, my own ephemeral awakening redirected my attention. All of those years of undergraduate and legal training; thousands of hours researching and writing during recent years as an author; and, the many hours of absorbing for pleasure historical biographies and metaphysics had resulted in a person whose vocabulary was inadequate.

One day a physician friend visited my office and used the word "paradigm". I was impressed. I did not know what it meant. After several years of these encounters, I decided to learn for myself the definition. It was apparent to me that if he knew that word, he must know many other words.

My "satchel of books and I" enjoy sitting on the beach under an umbrella from first light to sunset. Usually, I forget my pen. All of those words I could have noted and researched but did not. The challenge of catching up and actually recording, learning and being able to utilize the special words of our language seemed overwhelming. After all, there were just too many complex words out there. And it would be almost impossible to locate the perfect word. Common dictionaries do provide definitions, yet multiple word definitions cannot be categorized, and dictionaries omit the greatest words. Thesauri unfortunately provide multiple and confusing options, and they too usually omit the ultimate word.

In our frenetic society, there has occurred an aversion to writing utilizing compound and complex sentences and the use of words beyond the eighth grade level. Editors encourage reporters to write to be understood as do teachers of English. We are left to muse as to why America has not produced a Lincoln since Lincoln or a Jefferson since Jefferson. For students of English to include the multiple commas within their pages as did Lincoln and to reason beautifully as did Jefferson would effect some wrath from the instructor.

My grandparents, during the final years of the nineteenth century and the early years of the twentieth century, wrote beautiful letters to their children. Regrettably, today the art of meaningful, and, might I add, passionate writing almost is lost. One hope is the innumerable e-mails flashing through the ethos. However, such lingo, which is the abbreviated e-mail writing form, further has abridged expressed thought.

Finally, some years ago I did determine to begin recording for myself great words with simple definitions. A daily list was compiled and a total of three hundred fifty words resulted. But, how many more great words were out there? How could they be found, and could they be defined ever so simply with just one simple word? Hundreds of thousands of additional words were reviewed; and, astonishingly, amongst all of the words of the English language, only about fifteen hundred were determined worthy to add to my original list.

The process of defining complex words by a single word has been revolutionary. This is the key, the simple one word definition. This process has been mastered and can be utilized specifically to lead the searcher to great words. The simple one word index is the secret to capturing words of Shakespeare, Wordsworth and Longfellow.

While most complex words are well defined by common words, some are not, and you will just have to find those on your own. For others, effecting one word definitions necessitated "definitional" words of divergent grammatical types or word forms from respective counterparts. The one word definition for most words is "spot on", while the definitions of several of the words listed in this book are generic.

One of the more interesting thought processes in arriving at one word definitions was the quest for the definition of "animadversion". This word is defined otherwise as "aspersion", and I did not know what that meant. "Aspersion" is defined otherwise as "calumny", and I did not know what that meant. "Calumny" is defined otherwise as "slander". Finally, a word I could understand. Accordingly, each of these three words is defined in this book by the simple word "slander".

In the end, most words in the English language have a number of meanings. It was my attempt and based on my own experience, to effect my own subjectivity and judgment in an attempt to bring to the reader the most common, simple, generic and encompassing word, known and under-stood by most of us as the definitive word for the brilliant word to be mastered.

I challenge the reader to learn every word. It can be accom-plished in a year by memorizing six words daily. But, as you know, you will forget those words, so you must have a system. Each day you must not only learn six words, but you must re-view a number of words which you previously have learned. This process requires but several minutes a day.

Please remember these truths: (1) There are less than two thousand reasonably usable beautiful and complex words in the English language. (2) Most of these words have now been defined for you by a simple word. (3) Even a simple mind like mine and a great mind like yours can commit these words to memory and use them.

For the most part, "terms of art" such as scientific, medical, legal and words specific to other realms have been omitted. Several of these words are included if they are words reason-ably applicable in daily life.

Book I, COMPLEX WORDS to common words, invites the reader to absorb and enjoy the richness of alphabetized com-plex words. Book II, common words to COMPLEX WORDS, pro-vides the unique, all-important access, via one word definitions, to 1847 beautifully complex words of highly effective people.

Now, allow your world, your mind, emotions and passions, to accept a new and powerful gift-the most mellifluous, gran-diloquent words of the language called English.

■

BOOK I

COMPLEX WORDS to common words

CHAPTER
A

AASVOGEL	....	vulture
ABDOMINOUS	....	overweight
ABECEDARIAN	....	beginner
ABIRRITANT	....	soothing
ABJECT	....	depressed
ABJURATION	....	perjury
ABJURE	....	renounce
ABLACTATION	....	weaning
ABLATE	....	remove
ABLEPSIA	....	blindness

ABL: ## ACI:

ABLUTION	....	washing
ABNEGATION	....	renunciation
ABOREOUS	....	wooded
ABRADE	....	criticize
ABRECTION	....	catharsis
ABSCISSION	....	remove
ABSQUATULATE	....	escape
ABSTERMIOUS	....	moderation
ABSTRACT	....	apart
ABSTRUSE	....	confusing
ACCELERANDO	....	quickening-music
ACCOUCHEMENT	....	birthing
ACCOUTER	....	cloth
ACCOUTREMENT	....	accessory
ACCRESCENT	....	enlarged
ACERBIC	....	unruly
ACEROSE	....	needlelike
ACESCENT	....	sour
ACICULAR	....	needlelike
ACIDULOUS	....	biting

ACL:		**ADV:**
ACLIVITY	....	ascending
ACORIA	....	ravenous
ACRASIA	....	weak
ACRETION	....	growth
ACRID	....	bitter
ACRIMONY	....	harshness
ACROMEGALY	....	giantness
ACULEATE	....	direct
ADAGIO	....	ballet-duet
ADAMANTINE	....	hard
ADIPOSITY	....	obesity
ADJURE	....	implore
ADJUVANT	....	contributory
ADNEXA	....	appendages
ADSCITITIOUS	....	more
ADULATORY	....	flatter
ADULTERATE	....	contaminate
ADUMBRAL	....	shadowy
ADUMBRATE	....	intimate
ADVENTITIOUS	....	accidental

AEGIS	....	sponsorship
AELUROPHILE	....	cat-lover
AERATE	....	ventilate
AERUGINOUS	....	blue
AESCENT	....	damp
AFEBRILE	....	feverless
AFFLATUS	....	motivation
AFFRIGHTED	....	afraid
AFFUSION	....	pour
AGAMOGENESIS	....	asexual
AGAMOUS	....	single
AGENESIA	....	sterility
AGRESTIC	....	crude
ALACRITY	....	cheerful
ALARUMS	....	martial
ALBESCENT	....	whitish
ALEATORIC	....	luck
ALEATORY	....	random
ALEXIA	....	illiterate
ALGIDITY	....	coldness

ALI: AMP:

ALIMENT	....	food
ALIMENTARY	....	nourishing
ALIQUOT	....	fractional
ALLEGORICAL	....	figuratively
ALLIACEOUS	....	oniony
ALOPECIA	....	hairless
ALVEOLUS	....	cavity
AMALGAMATION	....	merge
AMANUENSIS	....	transcriber
AMATIVE	....	amorous
AMATORY	....	sexual
AMBIENT	....	surrounding
AMBUSCADE	....	ambush
AMBUSTION	....	burn
AMELIORATE	....	improve
AMENITY	....	agreeable
AMERCEMENT	....	fine
AMORETTO	....	cupid
AMORPHOUS	....	shapeless
AMPHIBOLOGY	....	unclear

AMPHIGORY	....	unclear
AMPLYOPIA	....	dimness
AMULET	....	charm
ANABASIS	....	advance
ANABATIC	....	rising
ANACHRONISM	....	inchronological
ANACREONTIC	....	adoring
ANADIPSIA	....	thirst
ANAGOGIC	....	mystical
ANAGRAM	....	rearrange
ANALITY	....	perfection
ANALOG	....	analogous
ANAMNESIS	....	remember
ANAMORPHOSIS	....	distorted
ANASTOMOSIS	....	joining
ANATHEMA	....	curse
ANATOMIZE	....	analyze
ANCHORET	....	recluse
ANCHORITE	....	hermit
ANCILLA	....	accessory

ANC: ANT:

ANCIPITAL	....	two-edged
ANDROGYNOUS	....	bisexual
ANECDOTAL	....	story
ANFRACTUOUS	....	sinuous
ANILE	....	senile
ANIMADVERSION	....	slander
ANIMUS	....	spirit
ANNALIST	....	historian
ANNULAR	....	ring-shaped
ANODYNE	....	anesthetic
ANOMALY	....	irregularity
ANSERINE	....	unwise
ANTEDILUVIAN	....	ancient
ANTHOLOGY	....	epigrams
ANTHROPOID	....	ape
ANTHROPOMORPHIC	....	humanistic
ANTHROPOPHAGY	....	cannibalism
ANTIPATHY	....	dislike
ANTIPHONAL	....	responsive
ANTIPHRASTIC	....	different

ANT: APO:

ANTIQUARIAN	....	collector
ANTITHESIS	....	opposite
ANUROUS	....	tailless
APERCUS	....	insight
APERIENT	....	laxative
APERTURE	....	opening
APHASIA	....	incomprehension
APHORISM	....	truth
APHOTIC	....	dark
APHRODISIAC	....	sexual
APICULATE	....	pointed
APOCATASTASIS	....	restoration
APOCRYPHAL	....	false
APODICTIC	....	irrefutable
APOETHM	....	saying
APOGEE	....	culmination
APOGRAPH	....	copy
APOLAUSTIC	....	pleasure
APOPLECTIC	....	stroke
APOSTASY	....	disloyalty

APOTHEGM	....	saying
APOTHEOSIS	....	ideal
APPANAGE	....	grant
APPELLATION	....	name
APPETENCE	....	want
APPOSITE	....	pertinent
APPURTENANCE	....	adjunct
APPURTENANT	....	accompanying
AQUILINE	....	curved
ARCANE	....	mysterious
ARCHETYPAL	....	original
ARCHETYPE	....	original
ARENOSE	....	sandy
ARGENT	....	silver
ARGOT	....	slang
ARPEGGIO	....	chord
ARRANT	....	shameless
ARROGATE	....	appropriate
ARTIFICE	....	trick
ASCETIC	....	self-denial

ASCRIPTION	....	attribute
ASEPTIC	....	germless
ASEXUALIZATION	....	sterilize
ASPERITY	....	roughness
ASPERSION	....	slander
ASSEVERATE	....	proclaim
ASSIDUOUS	....	diligent
ASSIGNATION	....	appointment
ASSUAGE	....	satisfy
ASSURGENT	....	rising
ASTHENIC	....	weak
ASTRINGENT	....	constrictive
ASYMPTOTE	....	tangent
ATARACTIC	....	calm
ATAVISM	....	throwback
ATAVISTIC	....	parent-like
ATELIER	....	studio
ATHANASIA	....	immortality
ATHWART	....	across
ATRABILIOUS	....	gloomy

ATTENUATE	....	weaken
AUBERGINE	....	eggplant-color
AUDACIOUS	....	bold
AUGMENT	....	enlarge
AUGURY	....	prophecy
AULIC	....	courtly
AUSCULTATION	....	hearing
AUSTERE	....	stern
AUTARKY	....	independence
AUTOCHTHONOUS	....	native
AUTOCLAVE	....	sterilize
AUTODIDACT	....	self-educated
AUTODIDACTIC	....	self-taught
AUTOEROTISM	....	self-arousal
AUTOGENOUS	....	independently
AUTOLOGOUS	....	independently
AUTOMATON	....	mechanical
AVARICIOUS	....	greedy
AVATAR	....	son-of-God
AVIDITY	....	greed

AVU: AXI:

AVULSION	....	tearing
AVUNCULAR	....	uncle-like
AWRY	....	deviating
AXIOMATIC	....	true

CHAPTER
B

BACCHANALIAN	....	drunken
BACILLUS	....	bacterium
BACULINE	....	rod-like
BADINAGE	....	teasing
BAGATELLE	....	trifle
BAGNIO	....	cathouse
BAITHE	....	concur
BALEFUL	....	harmful
BANAL	....	ordinary
BANAUSIC	....	ordinary

BAR: BIL:

BAROQUE	....	ornate
BARRATRY	....	litigious
BASTINADO	....	beating
BATHOS	....	sentimentality
BATTRICE	....	divide
BEATIFIC	....	bliss
BEDIZEN	....	gaudy
BELAY	....	stop
BEMUSE	....	confuse
BENIGNANT	....	kind
BENISON	....	blessing
BERCEUSE	....	lullaby
BESEEM	....	suitable
BESOM	....	sweeper
BESPANGLE	....	sprinkle
BIBLIOPHILE	....	book-collector
BIBLIOPOLE	....	bookseller
BIBULOUS	....	absorbent
BIFURCATE	....	divide
BILLINGSGATE	....	vulgarity

BIN: BUB:

BIN		BUB
BINATE	....	pairs
BISQUE	....	soupy
BLITHE	....	merry
BLOVIATE	....	verbose
BOEOTIAN	....	stupid
BOISRERIE	....	wood-carved
BOMBINATE	....	hum
BOOBOISIE	....	uneducated
BORBORYEM	....	flatulence
BOURGEOIS	....	middleclass
BOSCAGE	....	trees
BOWDLERIZE	....	cleanse
BRACHYLOGY	....	concise
BRADYCARDIA	....	slow-heart
BRAIDISM	....	hypnotism
BRANNIGAN	....	drinking
BREASTWORK	....	fortification
BREVETTED	....	ranked
BROBDINGNAGIAN	....	huge
BUBULCITATA	....	cowboyish

BUC: BUS:

BUCCAL	....	cheek
BUCENTAUR	....	barge
BUCOLIC	....	rustic
BUMPTIOUS	....	self-assertive
BUSKY	....	wooded

CHAPTER
C

CABAL	....	plotters
CACHE	....	storage
CADAVEROUS	....	ghastly
CADGE	....	borrow
CACHEXIA	....	ill-health
CACHINNATE	....	laugh
CACODEMON	....	evil-spirit
CACOPHONY	....	harsh
CADUCOUS	....	brief
CAIRN	....	memorial

CALABASH	....	gourd
CALDERA	....	crater
CALEFACIENT	....	heating
CALIGINOUS	....	dark
CALUMET	....	pipe
CALUMNY	....	slander
CAMPESTRAL	....	rural
CAMSTAIRY	....	stubborn
CANARD	....	lie
CANICAL	....	music
CANESCENT	....	grayish
CANNULAR	....	tubular
CANONICAL	....	conforming
CANROUS	....	melodic
CANT	....	insincerity
CANTON	....	division
CANTONMENT	....	quarters
CAPACIOUS	....	roomy
CAPIAS	....	warrant
CAPONIZE	....	alter

CAP: ## CEN:

CAP:		CEN:
CAPRICIOUS	....	impulsive
CAPTIOUS	....	faultfinding
CARCELAGE	....	free
CARCINOMA	....	cancer
CARNIVOROUS	....	meat-eater
CARPING	....	complaining
CARTOGRAPHER	....	mapper
CASEOUS	....	cheesy
CASHIER	....	dismiss
CASTELLATED	....	turreted
CASTIGATE	....	criticize
CASUISTICAL	....	rationalist
CASUISTRY	....	dishonesty
CATENATE	....	link
CAVEAT	....	warning
CAVIL	....	quibble
CELERITY	....	speed
CEMENTITIOUS	....	hard
CENSORIOUS	....	critical
CENTRIPETAL	....	inward

CERULEAN	....	azure
CERUMEN	....	earwax
CHAMPERTOUS	....	joining
CHAMPIGNON	....	mushroom
CHARINESS	....	caution
CHARY	....	shy
CHAUVINISM	....	unreasonable
CHIMERA	....	illusion
CHIMERICAL	....	imaginary
CHIROGRAPHY	....	penmanship
CHTHONIC	....	ghostly
CHOLERIC	....	irritable
CHOPLOGIC	....	disputing
CHURLISH	....	boorish
CICERONE	....	guide
CINCTURE	....	belt
CIRCUMFERENTIALLY	....	circle-like
CIRCUMFLUENT	....	flowing
CIRCUMLOCUTION	....	wordiness
CIRCUMSCRIPTION	....	definition

CIRCUMVOLUTION	....	revolve
CLARY	....	cautious
CLAUDICATION	....	limping
CLERESTORY	....	gallery
CLIMACTERIC	....	crucial
CLOCHARD	....	vagrant
CLOISTRESS	....	nun
CLOTURE	....	end
COAPTATION	....	fasten
COCKADE	....	knot
CODICIL	....	supplement
COEFFICIENT	....	number
COEVAL	....	contemporanious
COGENT	....	convincing
COGNATE	....	kin
COGNOMEN	....	surname
COGNOSCENTE	....	expert
COLLET	....	collar
COLLEGIALITY	....	power-sharing
COLLOCATE	....	place-together

COL:		CON:
COLUMBARIUM	....	niches
COLORABLE	....	believable
COMEDO	....	blackhead
COMESTIBLE	....	eatable
COMITY	....	courteous
COMMINATION	....	vengeance
COMMODIOUS	....	roomy
COMPENDIUM	....	summary
COMPLAISANT	....	agreeable
COMPORTMENT	....	behavior
COMPUNCTION	....	remorse
CONCATENATION	....	integration
CONCERTATION	....	assistance
CONCINNITY	....	harmony
CONCINNOUS	....	well-dressed
CONCOMITANT	....	accompanying
CONCUPISCENCE	....	sexuality
CONCUPISCENT	....	sexual
CONDIGN	....	merited
CONDOTTIERE	....	mercenary

CONEPATE	....	skunk
CONFABULATE	....	chat
CONFLATION	....	blend
CONFUTATION	....	disputation
CONGERIES	....	pile
CONIFER	....	evergreen
CONJURE	....	adjure
CONNUBIAL	....	marital
CONODONT	....	fossil
CONQEABLE	....	legal
CONSANGUINITY	....	blood-relation
CONSENTANEOUS	....	agreeing
CONSERVATORY	....	school-of-arts
CONSONANCE	....	accord
CONSPECTUS	....	digest
CONSTUPRATE	....	rape
CONSUBSTANTIATE	....	proclaim
CONSUETUDINARY	....	customary
CONTERMINOUS	....	contiguous
CONTESTATION	....	dispute

CON: COU:

CONTINENCE	....	chastity
CONTRATEMPS	....	embarrassment
CONTUMACIOUS	....	disobedient
CONTUMELIOUS	....	embarrassing
CONURBATION	....	urbanization
CONUNDRUM	....	riddle
CONVIVIAL	....	friendly
COOPTION	....	election
COPROLALIA	....	obscenities
COQUETTISH	....	flirt
CORPOSANT	....	fireball
CORPULENT	....	fat
CORRIGENDUM	....	error
CORSAIR	....	pirate
CORUSATE	....	sparkle
CORUSCATION	....	bright
CORYBANTIC	....	frenzied
COSTREL	....	flask
COTERIE	....	group
COUCHANT	....	prone

COUNTERMINOUS	....	adjoining
COUNTERVAIL	....	compensate
COURTESAN	....	prostitute
COZEN	....	cheat
CRAPULENCE	....	gluttonous
CRAPULOUS	....	glutton
CRASSITUDE	....	dumb
CRAVEN	....	coward
CREPUSCULAR	....	low-light
CREPUSCULE	....	evening
CRIBRIFORM	....	perforated
CROTCHETY	....	whim
CRYPTESTHESIA	....	mind-reader
CRYPTIC	....	puzzling
CUMSHAN	....	gratuity
CUNCTATION	....	postpone
CUNCTATIVE	....	procrastinator
CUNCTIPOTENT	....	all-powerful
CUPIDINOUS	....	greedy
CUPIDITY	....	greed

CUR: **CYN:**

CURMUDGEON	....	disagreeable
CUSHAT	....	pigeon
CUSTUMAL	....	lawbook
CYCLOPEAN	....	huge
CYNOSURE	....	show-off

CHAPTER
D

DAEDUL	....	skillful
DANDLE	....	dance
DEALBATION	....	bleaching
DEASIL	....	clockwise
DECAMP	....	move
DECIDUOUS	....	hardwood
DECLIVITY	....	downward
DECOLLETAGE	....	neckline
DECRESCENT	....	ending
DECUSSATE	....	crossing

DEDIFFERENTICTION	....	change
DEESIS	....	prayer
DEFALCATION	....	embezzlement
DEFENESTRATE	....	throwout
DEFFERVESCENCE	....	boil
DEFLAGRATE	....	burn
DEFLORATION	....	ravishing
DEGLUTITION	....	swallowing
DEICTIC	....	proving
DEIPNOSOPHIST	....	communicative
DELASSATION	....	exhausted
DELECTATION	....	pleasure
DELIQUESCE	....	melt
DELUSIVE	....	deceptive
DEMIGOD	....	godman
DEMIMONDE	....	prostitutes
DEMULCENT	....	soothing
DEMURRAGE	....	hold-up
DENDROPHILOUS	....	tree-like
DENOUEMENT	....	revelation

DEN: ## DIA:

DENUDE	....	strip
DEONTOLOGY	....	morality
DEPILATE	....	hair-removal
DERACINATE	....	uproot
DERGE	....	generals
DERRECLATIONS	....	plunder
DESICCATE	....	dried
DESIDERATE	....	wishful
DESUETUDE	....	disuse
DESULTORY	....	random
DETERGE	....	wash
DETRITUS	....	pieces
DETUMESCENCE	....	reduction
DEUTEROPATHY	....	unusual
DEVOLUTION	....	degeneration
DEXTRAL	....	right-handed
DIADEM	....	headband
DIALECTIC	....	debate
DIALECTIC	....	logical
DIAPHANOUS	....	transparent

DIA: DIS:

DIATRIBE	....	criticism
DICHOTOMY	....	division
DIDACTIC	....	teach
DIFFIDENT	....	reserved
DILATANTE	....	superficial
DIMINUTIVE	....	tiny
DIONISM	....	homosexuality
DIPSOMANIAC	....	alcoholic
DISABUSED	....	errorless
DISAMENITY	....	unfortunate
DISAPPROBATION	....	disapproval
DISCALCED	....	shoeless
DISCERP	....	rip
DISCERPTIBLE	....	partitionable
DISCOMFITURE	....	embarrassment
DISCRETE	....	separate
DISCURSIVE	....	rambling
DISESTABLISH	....	terminate
DISGORGE	....	unload
DISHABILLE	....	disarray

DIS:

DOW:

DISIDENCE	....	dissent
DISINGENUOUS	....	insincere
DISPARATE	....	distinct
DISPITEOUS	....	cruel
DISPUTATION	....	debate
DISSILIENT	....	erupting
DISSONANCE	....	discord
DISTRAITE	....	forgetful
DITHYRAMBIC	....	excited
DIURNAL	....	daily
DIVA	....	goddess
DIVAGATE	....	wander
DIVAGATION	....	digression
DOGGERAL	....	trival
DOLMEN	....	prehistoric
DOLOROUS	....	mournful
DOLTISH	....	stupid
DOTATION	....	endowment
DOUR	....	stern
DOWSABEL	....	sweetheart

DOY: DYS:

DOYEN	....	senior
DRAMATURGIC	....	theatrical
DRECK	....	inferior
DRIEGH	....	dreary
DRIVEL	....	dote
DROSS	....	waste
DUBIOSITY	....	uncertainty
DUDGEON	....	resentful
DUENNA	....	chaperone
DULCETLY	....	melodiously
DYAGENESIS	....	malformation
DYSOLISTIC	....	disdain
DYSPEPTIC	....	indigestion
DYSPHORIA	....	nervousness

CHAPTER
E

EBULLITION	....	bubbles
ECCHYMOSIS	....	bruise
ECCLESIA	....	audience
EDCYSIAST	....	stripper
ECHELONS	....	levels
ECHOPRAXIA	....	mimic
ECLECTIC	....	mixed
ECTOMORPHIS	....	slender
EDACIOUS	....	gluttonous
EDUCE	....	pull-out

EFFLEURAGE	....	rubbing
EFFLICACIOUS	....	effective
EFFLORESCENCE	....	fulfillment
EFFLUENCE	....	flowing
EFFLUVIUM	....	smelly
EFFRONTERY	....	nerve
EFFRONTUOUS	....	boldness
EFFULGENCE	....	brilliance
EFFULGENT	....	beaming
EGALITARIAN	....	equality
EGREGIOUS	....	horrible
EIDETIC	....	memorizable
EIDOLON	....	imaginary
ELAN	....	spirited
ELDRITCH	....	weird
ELEEMOSYNARY	....	charitable
ELEGICAL	....	mournful
ELEGY	....	poem
ELENCHUS	....	dispute
ELEPHANTIASIS	....	enlargement

ELO:

ENS:

ELOCUTION	....	speaking
ELYSIAN	....	blissful
EMASCULATE	....	weaken
EMBOUCHURE	....	mouth
EMEND	....	edit
EMOLLIENT	....	relaxing
EMOLUMENT	....	salary
EMPIRICAL	....	verification
EMPYREAN	....	heaven
ENCOMIUMS	....	praise
ENCOPRESIS	....	eliminate
ENCUMBRANCE	....	burden
ENDEMIC	....	localized
ENDOGENOUS	....	independently
ENIGMA	....	confusing
ENISLE	....	isolate
ENNUI	....	boredom
ENSCONCED	....	sheltered
EMSEMBLE	....	performers
ENSORCEL	....	bewitch

ENTELECHY	....	awakening
ENTOIL	....	trap
ENTROPY	....	disorder
EPHEMERAL	....	short-lived
EPICENE	....	effeminate
EPICUREAN	....	pleasurable
EPIGONE	....	inferior
EPIGRAM	....	saying
EPIGRAMMATIC	....	concise
EPIPHANY	....	awakening
EPISTOLARY	....	letters
EPITHET	....	disparagement
EPITHYMY	....	passionate
EQUABLE	....	steady
EQUIPAGE	....	horse-drawn
EQUIPONDERANT	....	balanced
EQUIPOLLENT	....	equivalent
EQUIVOQUE	....	pun
EREMITE	....	hermit
ERETHISM	....	stimulation

ERISTIC	....	argumentative
EROGENOUS	....	arousing
ERSATZ	....	artificial
ERUCT	....	belch
ERUCTATE	....	burp
ERUDITION	....	scholarship
ERUMPENT	....	thrusting
ESCALADE	....	scale
ESCARPMENT	....	cliff
ESCHATOLOGY	....	afterlife
ESCHEAT	....	confiscate
ESCLUENT	....	edible
ESCRITOIRE	....	desk
ESCULENT	....	digestible
ESCUTCHEON	....	shield
ESOTERIC	....	confidential
ESPIEGLE	....	playful
ESPLANADE	....	plain
ESURIENT	....	greedy
ETATISM	....	socialism

ETERNE	....	everlasting
ETESIAN	....	yearly
ETHEREAL	....	airy
ETHNOCENTRICITY	....	racism
ETIOLATE	....	whiten
ETIOLOGY	....	cause
EUDEMONIA	....	happiness
EUPHUISTIC	....	eloquent
EUTETIC	....	thaw
EVANESCE	....	vanish
EVISCERATE	....	deprive
EXCELSIOR	....	shavings
EXCLAMATION	....	explanation
EXCORIATE	....	criticize
EXCREMENTITIOUS	....	feces
EXCRESCENCE	....	wart
EXCULPATE	....	acquit
EXCURSIVE	....	meandering
EXECRATED	....	detested
EXECRATIVE	....	detestable

EXEGESIS	....	explanation
EXEGETICAL	....	explanatory
EXIGENCY	....	urgency
EXIGUOUS	....	meager
EXIMIOUS	....	excellent
EXISTENTIAL	....	verification
EXORDIUM	....	beginning
EXPATIATING	....	talkative
EXPIATE	....	atone
EXPONENT	....	symbol
EXPOSE	....	exposure
EXPOSTULATE	....	object
EXPOSTULATION	....	objection
EXPURGATE	....	edit
EXPURGATE	....	remove
EXTIRPATE	....	destroy
EXTIRPATION	....	removal
EXTRAPOLATE	....	speculate
EXTRAVASATE	....	effluence

CHAPTER
F

FACILE	....	accomplishable
FACINOROUS	....	wicked
FACTITIOUS	....	artifical
FACTOTUM	....	servant
FACULTATIVE	....	authority
FAINEANT	....	lazy
FANFARON	....	braggart
FANION	....	flag
FARCEUR	....	joker
FARDEL	....	encumbrance

FARINALEOUS	....	starchy
FASTNESS	....	stronghold
FATIDIC	....	prophetic
FATUOUS	....	foolish
FAUTEUIL	....	armchair
FAUXER	....	forge
FEALTY	....	fidelity
FECKLESS	....	worthless
FECULENT	....	foul
FECUND	....	fertile
FECUNDITY	....	fertility
FELICITOUS	....	pleasant
FEMME FATALE	....	seductive
FENESTRATED	....	pierced
FERAL	....	natural
FERITY	....	wildness
FERRIAGE	....	fare
FERVID	....	zealous
FESTINATE	....	hastening
FETID	....	stinking

FET: FOR:

FETTED	....	praised
FILCH	....	steal
FISTULA	....	passage
FIVER	....	money
FLACCID	....	limp
FLACETIOUS	....	flippant
FLAGELLATE	....	whip
FLAGITIOUS	....	wicked
FLAMBEAU	....	flaming
FLABUGINOUS	....	false
FLECHE	....	steeple
FLEER	....	laugh
FLIVER	....	car
FLORID	....	flowery
FLUMMOXED	....	confused
FLUMMERY	....	flattery
FLURRIED	....	agitated
FOMENTER	....	troublemaker
FORFEND	....	avert
FORSWEAR	....	renounce

FRA: FUS:

FRACTIOUS	....	quarrelsome
FRANGIBLE	....	fragile
FRENETIC	....	frantic
FRISSON	....	thrill
FROIDEUR	....	stuck-up
FROUFROU	....	swishing
FROWSTY	....	musty
FUGACIOUS	....	fleeting
FULGURATION	....	flash
FULIGINOUS	....	smoky
FULMINATE	....	denunciation
FULSOME	....	disgusting
FUMAROLE	....	vent
FUNDAMENT	....	buttocks
FUNEREAL	....	mournful
FUNGIBLE	....	indistinguishable
FURCIFEROUS	....	disgustingly
FURTIVELY	....	stealthily
FUSCOUS	....	lightless
FUSILLADE	....	gunfire

| FUSTIAN | .... | exaggerated |
| FUSTIGATE | .... | punish |

CHAPTER
G

GAINSAY	....	deny
GALIMATIAS	....	confused
GALLIVANT	....	wander
GALVANIC	....	electric
GARRULITY	....	talkative
GARRULOUS	....	talkative
GASCONADING	....	boasting
GAUCHE	....	tactless
GELID	....	chilly
GENRE	....	style-of-writing

GEN: GRA:

GENUFLECT	....	bend
GEODESIC	....	straight
GEOPONIC	....	agrarian
GERARCHY	....	hierarchy
GLABROUS	....	smooth
GLISSADE	....	glide
GLOAMING	....	twilight
GLOBOUS	....	spherical
GLOSSOLALIA	....	unintelligible
GNATHONIC	....	flattering
GNOSIS	....	mysticism
GOMERAL	....	fool
GORMLESS	....	stupid
GOURMAND	....	glutton
GRACILE	....	thin
GRAMARYE	....	magic
GRAMINEOUS	....	grassy
GRANDILOQUENCE	....	bombastic
GRATULANCE	....	bribe
GRAVAMEN	....	essential

GRA: ## GUL:

GRAGARIOUS	....	friendly
GRENADINE	....	reddish-orange
GRIFTER	....	swindler
GROUSING	....	nagging
GUISLING	....	traitor
GULOSITOUS	....	gluttonous

CHAPTER
H

HABILIMENT	....	clothing
HALATION	....	blurred
HALCYON	....	calm
HARLEQUIN	....	comic
HAUTEUR	....	haughtiness
HAVEREL	....	fool
HEBDOMEDAL	....	weekly
HEBETUDE	....	dullness
HECTOR	....	swagger
HEDONISTIC	....	pleasurable

HEG: HIS:

HEGEMONY	....	authority
HEINIE	....	buttocks
HELICINE	....	spiral
HELIOCENTRIC	....	sun-centered
HELIOTROPE	....	purplish
HELIOSIS	....	sunstroke
HENGHEN	....	gale
HEREDITAMENT	....	inheritance
HERMENEUTICS	....	interpretation
HERMETIC	....	magical
HETAERA	....	prostitute
HETEROCHTHONOUS	...	foreign
HETERODOX	....	unorthodox
HETEROGENEOUS	....	mixed
HEURISTIC	....	teaching
HIERATIC	....	priently
HIRCINE	....	lustful
HIRSUTE	....	hairy
HISTOGENSIS	....	growth
HISTRIONIC	....	theatrical

HOL: HYP:

HOLOGRAPHIC	....	self-written
HOMILY	....	sermon
HOMOEROTOCISM	....	homosexuality
HOMOGAMY	....	inbreeding
HOMOLOGATE	....	approve
HOMOLOGATION	....	confirmation
HOMUNCULUS	....	midget
HORTATIVE	....	encouraging
HOYDEN	....	tomboy
HUBRIS	....	pride
HUDERON	....	inactive
HYDROPHILIC	....	water-receptive
HYDROPHOBIC	....	water-repellant
HUMECTANT	....	wetting
HYPERBOLIC	....	exaggeration
HYPERBOREAN	....	frigid
HYPEREMESIS	....	vomiting
HYPNAGOGIC	....	sleepiness
HYPNOPEDIA	....	education
HYPOSTATIZE	....	externalize

HYPOTHECATE	....	pledge
HYPOTHESIS	....	theory
HYPOXIA	....	suffocation

CHAPTER
I

IATROGENIC	....	diseased
ICON	....	god-like
ICONOCLAST	....	rebellious
IDENTIC	....	same
IDEOGRAM	....	symbol
IDIOM	....	dialect
IDIOPATHIC	....	uncertain
IDIOSYNCRATIC	....	peculiarity
IDONEOUS	....	suitable
IGNEOUS	....	volcanic

IGNOSLENCY	....	pardon
ILLECEBROUS	....	good-looking
ILLIQUID	....	cashless
IMBROGLIO	....	entanglement
IMMEDICABLE	....	incurable
IMMISCIBLE	....	unmixable
IMMOLATE	....	sacrifice
IMMURED	....	walled-over
IMMUTABLE	....	unchangeable
IMPEDIMENTA	....	suitcase
IMPERCIPIENT	....	misunderstanding
IMPERIOUS	....	lordly
IMPERTURBATION	....	unflappable
IMPIGROUS	....	fact
IMPIOUS	....	idolatry
IMPOLITIC	....	rash
IMPONE	....	wager
IMPORTUNE	....	beg
IMPORTUNATE	....	solicit
IMPORUS	....	dense

IMPRECATION	....	curse
IMPRESARIO	....	conductor
IMPREST	....	loan
IMPROVIDENT	....	unprepared
IMPUDENCE	....	disregard
IMPUGNED	....	admonish
IMPUISSANCE	....	feeble
IMPUTRESCIBLE	....	moral
INALIENABLE	....	unsaleable
INAMORATA	....	lover
INANE	....	empty
INANITION	....	exhaustion
INCANTATION	....	chanting
INCHOATE	....	incomplete
INCIPIENT	....	awakening
INCIVISM	....	anti-government
INCOMMODIOUS	....	inconvenient
INCONSONANT	....	inconsistent
INCONY	....	pretty
INCORPOREAL	....	formless

INC: ## ING:

INCULPATE ···· blame

INCUBUS ···· nightmare

INCUNABULA ···· beginnings

INDAGATE ···· search

INDEFATIGABLE ···· tireless

INDIFFERENT ···· unbiased

INDIGENOUS ···· native

INDISCERPTIBLE ···· impartitionable

INDOLENT ···· lazy

INDULGENT ···· self-gratification

INDURATE ···· callous

INDURATED ···· hardened

INEFFABLE ···· unspeakable

INELUCTABLE ···· irresistible

INENARRABLE ···· self-sufficient

INERT ···· powerless

INEXORABLE ···· relentless

INFIDEL ···· unbeliever

INGANNATION ···· deceit

INGEMINATE ···· repeat

INGLORIOUS	....	shameful
INGRAVESCENT	....	worsening
INGUINAL	....	groin
INIMICAL	....	unfriendly
INIMITABLE	....	matchless
INIQUITOUS	....	wickedness
INNOCUOUS	....	harmless
INOSCULATE	....	joining
INSATIATE	....	insatiable
INSCRUTABLE	....	mysterious
INSENSATE	....	infatuated
INSIPID	....	tasteless
INSOLENT	....	rude
INSOUCIANT	....	lighthearted
INSPIRIT	....	encourage
INSPISSATED	....	thickened
INSUFFLATE	....	ventilate
INSULAR	....	local
INSURGENT	....	rebel
INTELLECTION	....	hold

INT: INV:

INTEMPERANCE	....	drunkard
INTERCALATE	....	insert
INTERCALATION	....	put-in
INTERDICT	....	destroy
INTERLOCUTION	....	conversation
INTERNECINE	....	kill
INTERNUNCIAL	....	proclaiming
INTERPOLATE	....	insert
INTERREGNUM	....	leaderless
INTERROGATORIES	....	questions
INTERSTICES	....	crevices
INTRACTABILITY	....	obstinate
INTRANSIGENT	....	uncompromising
INTREPID	....	fearless
INTROMIT	....	confess
INTUITED	....	understanding
INTUMESCENT	....	charing
INTUSSUSCEPT	....	enclose
INVAGINATE	....	enclose
INVECTIVE	....	insulting

INV: ITH:

INVEIGLE	....	flatter
INVETERATE	....	habitual
INVIDIOUS	....	obnoxious
INVIGILATION	....	observation
INVIGLE	....	entice
IRENIC	....	peaceful
IRRECUSABLE	....	reject
IRREDENTISM	....	inclusion
IRREFRAGABLE	....	irrefutable
IRREMEDIABLE	....	unsolvable
ISOMORPHIC	....	identical
ITERATION	....	repeating
ITHYPALLIC	....	lustful

CHAPTER
J

JACTATION	....	boasting
JACULATE	....	throw
JANISSARY	....	supporter
JECTIGATION	....	shaking
JEJUNE	....	unsatisfying
JINGOISM	....	chauvinism
JITNEY	....	bus
JOCUND	....	happy
JUNTO	....	revolution
JUVENESCENT	....	youthful
JUXTAPOSED	....	adjacent

CHAPTER
K

KARYOGAMY	....	nuclei
KEMP	....	champion
KIBOSH	....	stop
KINESIS	....	motion
KINETIC	....	motion
KINAESTHETIC	....	muscular
KINGBOLT	....	kingpin
KNOUT	....	knife
KVETCHY	....	complaining
KWAIKEN	....	knife

CHAPTER
L

LABEFACTION	....	revolution
LABILE	....	unstable
LABYRINTHIAN	....	winding
LACHES	....	delay
LACHRYMOSE	....	tearful
LACONIC	....	curt
LACRIMAL	....	tearing
LAETIFICANT	....	happy
LAMBENT	....	bright
LANCEOLATED	....	tapering

LANCINATING	....	stabbing
LANGUET	....	tongue
LANGUOR	....	sluggishness
LANGUOROUS	....	listless
LANUGINOUS	....	hairy
LAPACTIC	....	purging
LARBOARD	....	left
LARGESSE	....	generosity
LASCIVIOUS	....	lustful
LASSITUDE	....	fatigue
LEGERDEMAIN	....	slight-of-hand
LEGERITY	....	alacrity
LEGGIADROUS	....	polished
LEITMOTIF	....	recurring
LENITY	....	gentleness
LENTIGINOUS	....	spotted
LEUKOUS	....	white
LEVEE	....	reception
LEVIGATE	....	powderize
LEVIGATED	....	polished

LEX:		LOU:
LEXICON	....	dictionary
LIBIDINOUS	....	lustful
LICENTIOUSNESS	....	lewdness
LIEGE	....	loyal
LIGENOUS	....	wood-like
LILLIPUTIAN	....	small
LIMACINE	....	slug
LIMITROPHE	....	beside
LIMNED	....	draw
LIMPID	....	clear
LINEAMENT	....	outline
LIONIZATION	....	enhancement
LISSOME	....	nimble
LISTENABLE	....	considering
LITOTES	....	understatement
LITTORAL	....	shore
LONGANIMITY	....	patience
LOQUACIOUS	....	talkative
LOUCHE	....	shifty
LOUT	....	klutz

LOU: LYS:

LOUTISH	....	boorish
LUBRICIOUS	....	oily
LUCUBRATION	....	work
LUGUBRIOUS	....	mournful
LUXATION	....	dislocation
LYSIS	....	disappearance

CHAPTER
M

MACABRE	....	gruesome
MACERATE	....	soak
MACHINATION	....	plot
MACHONNEMENT	....	chewing
MACROBIOSIS	....	longevity
MACULATE	....	blemish
MAELSTROM	....	whirlpool
MAGNILOQUENT	....	bombastic
MAGNOLIOUS	....	hue
MAINSWORN	....	perjured

MAL: ## MAS:

MALADROIT	....	awkward
MALAPERT	....	bold
MALAPROPISMS	....	inappropriate
MALEDICTION	....	curse
MALEFACTOR	....	evildoer
MALEFIC	....	harmful
MALENTENDU	....	misunderstanding
MALEVOLENT	....	malicious
MALFACTOR	....	criminal
MALINGERER	....	faker
MALIORATIONS	....	improvements
MALODOROUS	....	stinking
MANDAMUS	....	command
MANDARIN	....	official
MANEGE	....	horsemanship
MANSUETUDE	....	gentleness
MANUDUCTION	....	instruction
MANUMISSION	....	emancipation
MANUMIT	....	free
MASOCHISM	....	self-deprivation

MAS: MET:

MASTICATE	....	chew
MATINAL	....	morning
MAUMET	....	idol
MAUNDER	....	wander
MAVIN	....	expert
MAWKISH	....	sentimental
MEGALOMANIA	....	self-possessed
MEGRIM	....	impulsive
MEIOSIS	....	understatement
MELANGE	....	mixture
MELLIFLUOUS	....	smoothly
MENDACIOUS	....	dishonest
MENDICANT	....	beggar
MENTITION	....	lie
MEPHITIC	....	poisonous
MEPHITIE	....	poisonous
MEPHITIS	....	blow-out
MERETRICIOUS	....	gaudy
MERITOCRACY	....	deserved
METALLOID	....	nonmetal

MET:		**MOL:**
METAPHYSICAL	....	philosophical
METASTASIZE	....	spread
METRONOMIC	....	regular
MIASMIC	....	poisonous
MICTURITION	....	urination
MILIEU	....	environment
MILLIARD	....	billion
MIMETIC	....	copying
MISANDROUS	....	hater
MISANTHROPIC	....	hater
MISASSAY	....	fail
MISAVER	....	misspeak
MISCREANT	....	villain
MISOGAMY	....	woman-hater
MNEMONIC	....	memory
MODERNITY	....	contemporary
MOIETY	....	half
MOLLIFY	....	pacify
MOLIMINOUS	....	hue
MOLLETON	....	cotton-cloth

MONIKER	....	name
MONILIFORM	....	beaded
MONTAGE	....	composite
MORDACIOUS	....	fussy
MORDANCY	....	sarcastic
MORDANT	....	biting
MORDOCIOUS	....	biting
MOREL	....	sponge
MORIBUND	....	dying
MORIGERATE	....	trustworthy
MORONIC	....	stupid
MOSCHATE	....	musky
MOUNTEBANK	....	pretender
MUCK	....	manure
MULIEBRITY	....	womanhood
MULISH	....	stubborn
MULTIFARIOUSNESS	....	diversity
MUNIFICENT	....	bountiful
MUNIMENT	....	defense
MUTABLE	....	changeable

MUT: ## MYZ:

MUTUATITIAL	....	loaned
MYRMIDON	....	henchman
MYRRHED	....	fragranced
MYTHOMANSIA	....	exaggerating
MYZESIS	....	sucking

CHAPTER
N

NABOBISM	....	wealth
NAOPLASM	....	tumor
NARCISSISM	....	self-love
NARCOMANIA	....	drug-addiction
NARCOSIS	....	unconsciousness
NARTHEX	....	vestibule
NASCENT	....	birthing
NATANT	....	floating
NAUFRAGATE	....	crash
NAUMACHY	....	sea-battle

NAUPATHIA	....	sea-sickness
NEBBISH	....	shy
NECESSITIOUS	....	urgent
NECROPOLIS	....	graveyard
NECROPSY	....	autopsy
NECROTIC	....	dead
NEFARIOUS	....	bad
NEOTERIC	....	new
NEOTERIC	....	young
NESCIENCE	....	ignorance
NEXUS	....	link
NICTITATE	....	blink
NIFFER	....	barter
NIHILISTIC	....	skepticism
NIMBUS	....	cloud
NIMIETY	....	redundancy
NIVEOUS	....	snow-like
NOCTAMBULIST	....	sleepwalker
NOCTULE	....	bat
NOCUOUS	....	harmful

NOD: NYX:

NODDY	....	fool
NOETIC	....	apart
NONPAREIL	....	peerless
NONPLUSSED	....	perplexed
NORMATIVE	....	standard
NOSTOMANIA	....	homesickness
NUBILE	....	attractive
NUGATORY	....	powerless
NUMINOUS	....	divine
NUMMULAR	....	coin-like
NUTATION	....	nodding
NYMPHOLEPSY	....	rapture
NYXIS	....	puncture

CHAPTER
O

OBACERATE	....	challenge
OBDURATE	....	inflexible
OBEISANT	....	respect
OBFUSCATE	....	confuse
OBIQUITY	....	indirectness
OBLATION	....	offering
OBLIVESCENCE	....	non-remembrance
OBLOQUY	....	disgrace
OBMUTESCENCE	....	mute
OBNUBILATE	....	darken

OBN: ODO:

OBNUBILATION	....	confused
OBREPTION	....	fraud
OBROGATION	....	annul
OBSCURANTISM	....	confusing
OBSECRATE	....	plead
OBSEQUIOUS	....	slavish
OBSEQUY	....	funeral-rite
OBSTIPATED	....	constipated
OBSTREPEROUSNESS	....	unruly
OBSTRICTION	....	obligation
OBTRUDE	....	thrust-out
OBTURATION	....	closing
OBTUSE	....	blunt
OBVIATE	....	prevent
OBVOLUTE	....	tuned-in
OCHLOCRACY	....	mob-rule
OCHLOCRATIC	....	riotous
ODALISQUE	....	concubine
ODIUM	....	hatred
ODONTALGIA	....	toothache

OEN:

ORE:

OENOLOGY	....	wine-study
OFACTION	....	smell
OFFAL	....	waste
OLEAGINOUS	....	oily
OLEOPHILIC	....	oil-receptive
OLEOPHOBIC	....	oil-repellent
OLIBANUM	....	perfume
ONOMATOPOEIA	....	sound-alike
OPALESCENT	....	iridescent
OPAQUE	....	lightless
OPEROSE	....	laborious
OPEROSENESS	....	boring
OPHIDIAN	....	snake
OPPROBRIUM	....	disgraceful
OPPUGN	....	assail
OPPUNGNANT	....	hostile
ORACULAR	....	inspired
ORDERMITION	....	numbness
ORDURE	....	waste
ORECTIC	....	desiring

ORG: OZO:

ORGULOUS	....	proud
ORIFICE	....	opening
ORISON	....	prayer
OSCITANT	....	yawn
OSCITATION	....	yawning
OSCULATION	....	kiss
OSMESIS	....	smelling
OSMOSIS	....	absorption
OSSIFY	....	harden
OTIOSE	....	idle
OULTREPREU	....	courageous
OXYMORONIC	....	incongruous
OZOSTOMIA	....	halitosis

CHAPTER
P

PACHYDERMATOUS	....	thick-skinned
PAEAN	....	praise
PAGINATE	....	number
PALABRA	....	word
PALAVER	....	chatter
PALEONTOLOGY	....	fossils
PALINGENETIC	....	rebirth
PALLIATIVE	....	ease
PALLIATE	....	conceal
PALUDISM	....	malaria

PAN: ## PAR:

PANACEA	....	cure-all
PANDEMIC	....	diseased
PANEGYRIC	....	eulogy
PANJANDRUM	....	pretender
PANOPLY	....	covering
PANTAGRUELISM	....	temperment
PANTHEISM	....	gods-in-nature
PANTHEON	....	temple-of-gods
PAOXYSM	....	fit
PARACLETE	....	advocate
PARAGON	....	model
PARADIGM	....	pattern
PARALOGISM	....	falsehood
PARAPET	....	wall
PARCENARY	....	joint
PARESTHESIAS	....	tingling
PARLOUS	....	dangerous
PARODY	....	imitation
PARONOMASIA	....	pun
PARSIMONIOUS	....	frugal

PARTITION	....	division
PARTURITION	....	childbirth
PASQUINADE	....	satire
PATERFAMILIAS	....	father
PATHOGEN	....	bacterium
PATHOGENIC	....	diseased
PATHOS	....	pity
PATRICIATE	....	aristocracy
PATRIMONY	....	inheritance
PATRONYMIC	....	surname
PATULOUS	....	exposed
PAVOR	....	fear
PECCABLE	....	mistake
PECULATION	....	embezzlement
PEDAGOGY	....	teaching
PEDANTIC	....	show-off
PEDERASTY	....	sodomy
PEDESTRIAN	....	commonplace
PEJORATIVE	....	disparaging
PELAGIC	....	oceanic

PELLUCID	....	transparent
PENSTER	....	writer
PENULTIMATE	....	next-to-last
PENURIOUS	....	stingy
PENURY	....	poor
PERADVENTURE	....	perhaps
PERAMENE	....	pleasing
PERCHANCE	....	perhaps
PERCUNCTORILY	....	inactive
PERDITION	....	hell
PERDURE	....	last
PEREGRINATE	....	walk
PEREGRINATION	....	journey
PERFERID	....	zealous
PERFIDY	....	faithless
PERFORCE	....	coercion
PERIPHRASTIC	....	roundabout
PERJURIOUS	....	lying
PERIGEE	....	culmination
PERIPATETIC	....	itinerant

PERIPHRASIS	....	wordy
PERIPHRASTIC	....	meandering
PERMEABLE	....	porous
PERNICIOUS	....	destructive
PERORATION	....	conclusion
PERSIFLAGE	....	banter
PERSPICACIOUS	....	understanding
PERTINACIOUS	....	tenacious
PERUKE	....	wig
PERVIGILIUM	....	wakefulness
PERVIOUS	....	accessible
PESTIFEROUS	....	annoying
PETCOCK	....	value
PETTIFOG	....	quibble
PHANTASMOGORIA	....	visions
PHILIFORM	....	hair-like
PHILIPPIC	....	invective
PHLEGMATIC	....	impassive
PHONOPHOBIC	....	sound-avoidance
PHOTOPHOBIC	....	light-avoidance

PIACULAR	....	sinful
PICARESQUE	....	scoundrel
PICAROON	....	robber
PIEBALD	....	spotted
PIED	....	multi-colored
PILOSE	....	hairy
PILPUL	....	hairsplitting
PINGUID	....	fat
PIQUANT	....	spicy
PISCATOR	....	fisherman
PISHOGUE	....	curse
PISMIRE	....	ant
PITYALISM	....	salivating
PLANGENT	....	loud
PLAUSIVE	....	praising
PLENIPOTENTIARY	....	diplomat
PLENITUDINOUS	....	fat
PLEONEXIA	....	covetous
PLUPERFECT	....	extraordinary
PLUVIAN	....	rainy

PLU:		POS:
PLUVIOUS	....	precipitating
POCOCURANTISH	....	neglectful
POETASTER	....	poet
POGONOLOGY	....	beards-study of
POLEMICAL	....	debative
POLITY	....	government
POLTROUN	....	coward
POLYDIPSIA	....	thirsty
POLYGOT	....	multilingual
POLYHISTOR	....	scholar
POLYMORPHOUS	....	many-stages
POLYONYMOUS	....	aliases
POLYPHAGIA	....	glutinous
POLYSTICHOUS	....	series
POPINJAY	....	talkative
PORCINE	....	piggish
PORTENTOUS	....	foreshadowing
PORTMANTEAU	....	suitcase
POSIT	....	assume
POSTICHE	....	false

POS: PRE:

POSTPRANDIAL	....	after-dinner
POSTULANT	....	novice
POTHER	....	fuss
PRATE	....	chatter
PRECIOSITY	....	tastefulness
PRECIPITOUS	....	steep
PRECONIZE	....	compliment
PRECOSIOUS	....	advanced
PREDACEOUS	....	stalking
PREFATORY	....	preliminary
PREHENSILE	....	grasping
PREHENSION	....	grasping
PREMONITARY	....	warning
PREPONDERANT	....	dominant
PREPOSSION	....	prejudice
PRESAGE	....	predict
PRESBYOPIA	....	farsighted
PRESCEND	....	separate
PRESCIENT	....	foreknowledge
PRETERNATURAL	....	supernatural

PRE: PRO:

PREVENIENT	....	anticipate
PRIAPIC	....	manly
PRIGGERY	....	theft
PRIGGISH	....	smug
PRIMORDIAL	....	original
PROBATIVE	....	proving
PROBITY	....	honest
PROBOSCIS	....	nose
PROCESVERBAL	....	record
PROCRUSTEAN	....	drastic
PROCUMBENT	....	lean
PROFANATION	....	blasphemy
PROFLIGACY	....	extravagant
PROFLUENT	....	smoothly
PROFUNDITY	....	profound
PROFUSE	....	lavish
PROGENITOR	....	ancestor
PROGENY	....	children
PROLEGOMENON	....	introductory
PROLEPIC	....	anticipate

PRO: **PUE:**

PROLIX	....	wordy
PROMULGE	....	proclaim
PROPHYLACTIC	....	preventative
PROPINQUITY	....	proximity
PROPITIATE	....	appease
PROPITIOUS	....	favorable
PROPOGATION	....	spreading
PROSAIC	....	dull
PROTEAN	....	chameleon
PROTUBERANT	....	spreading
PROTUBERATE	....	expand
PROVENANCE	....	source
PROVENDER	....	food
PROVENLY	....	doubtless
PRURIENT	....	sexual
PSELLISM	....	stutter
PSYCHOCOMA	....	stupor
PTARMUS	....	sneeze
PTYALORRHEA	....	salivate
PUERILE	....	childish

PUERLISM	....	childishness
PUGILIST	....	boxer
PUGNACIOUS	....	quarrelsome
PUISSANT	....	strong
PULCHRITUDE	....	beauty
PULCHRITUDINOUS	....	attractive
PULE	....	whine
PUNCTILIOUS	....	punctual
PUNDIT	....	intellect
PURLIEUS	....	limits
PURLOINED	....	stolen
PURULENT	....	pussy
PURVEYOR	....	supplier
PUSILLANIMOUS	....	cowardly
PUTON	....	hoax
PYROTIC	....	burning

CHAPTER
Q

QUADRENNIAL	....	fourth
QUARTERN	....	one-fourth
QUATERVOIS	....	intersection
QUEAN	....	prostitute
QUENNELLE	....	dumping
QUERULOUS	....	irritable
QUIDNUNC	....	busybody
QUINTESSENTIAL	....	typical
QUISLING	....	traitor
QUIXOTIC	....	impractical
QUOTIDIAN	....	ordinary

CHAPTER
R

RACINAGE	....	adorn
RACONTEUR	....	storyteller
RADICATE	....	rooting
RAILLERY	....	jest
RAKISH	....	jaunty
RAMOLLISSEMENT	....	softening
RAPACIOUS	....	ravenous
RAPPROCHEMENT	....	cordiality
RASPISH	....	irritable
RATIOCINATION	....	inference

RAV: 　　　　　　　　　　　　　　RED:

RAVISH	....	seize
REAGENT	....	initiator
REALPOLITIK	....	practical-politics
REBARBATIVE	....	irritating
REBORANT	....	strengthen
RECALCITRANT	....	stubborn
RECENSION	....	revision
RECHERCHE	....	unusual
RECIDIVISM	....	repeated
RECIPROCITY	....	mutuality
RECOGNIZANCE	....	pledge
RECONDITE	....	confusing
RECREANT	....	turncoat
RECRUDESCENCE	....	return
RECTITUDINOUS	....	moral
RECUMBENT	....	prone
RECUSANCY	....	denial
REDACT	....	edit
REDARQUE	....	disapprove
REDINTEGRATE	....	renovate

RED:		REP:
REDOLENT	....	fragrant
REDOUBT	....	fortification
REDOUBTABLE	....	dreaded
REDOUND	....	effective
REFULGENT	....	luminous
REIVE	....	plunder
RELEXIFICATION	....	translation
RELIQUARY	....	casket
RELUCENT	....	reflecting
REMIT	....	release
REMONSTRATE	....	object
RENAISSANCE	....	rebirth
RENDITION	....	extraction
RENITANCY	....	opposition
RENITENT	....	resistant
REPAIR	....	return
REPARATION	....	repay
REPARTITION	....	distribution
REPAST	....	meal
REPERTOIRE	....	performances

REPLETION	....	full
REPLEVY	....	regain
REPUGN	....	oppose
REREMICE	....	bats
RESECTION	....	remove
RESIDUUM	....	residue
RESILE	....	spring-back
RESTIVE	....	unruly
RETICULATED	....	netlike
RETINUE	....	followers
RETORTION	....	bend
RETROGRADE	....	backward
REVETMENTS	....	embankment
REVIVIFICATION	....	restore
REVIVIFY	....	restore
REYNARD	....	fox
RHABDOMANTIST	....	divination
RHAPHE	....	seam
RHONCUS	....	rale
RIBALD	....	profane

RIDDANCE	....	deliverance
RIPOSTE	....	insulting
RISIBLE	....	funny
RODOMONTADE	....	brag
ROENTGEN	....	x-ray
ROGATION	....	literary
ROGUE	....	scoundrel
ROISTER	....	revel
ROROGUE	....	discontinue
ROUSTABOUT	....	worker
RUBRIC	....	title
RUCTIOUS	....	quarrelsome
RUDIMENTARY	....	elementary
RUFESCENT	....	reddish
RUFUS	....	reddish
RUGOSE	....	wrinkled
RUMINATE	....	ponder
RUTILISM	....	redheaded

CHAPTER
S

SABULOUS	....	sandy
SACCADE	....	jerky
SACERDOTAL	....	priestly
SACHEM	....	leader
SAGACIOUS	....	perceptive
SAGACITY	....	wisdom
SAGITATE	....	triangular
SALACIOUS	....	lustful
SALEBROSITY	....	course
SALIENT	....	noticeable

SALTANT	....	dancing
SALUTARY	....	beneficial
SALVIFIC	....	saving
SANATIVE	....	healing
SANGFROID	....	imperturbable
SANGUINARY	....	bloody
SANGUINE	....	cheerful
SAPID	....	delicious
SAPIENCE	....	wisdom
SAPOR	....	flavor
SAPPHISM	....	lesbianism
SARCOLYTIC	....	decomposing
SARCOPHAGUS	....	coffin
SARCOUS	....	flesh
SARDONIC	....	sarcastic
SARTORIAL	....	tailored
SATIATE	....	satisfy
SATURINE	....	gloomy
SAULT	....	waterfall
SAVOIR FAIRE	....	tact

SCA: SED:

SCABROUS	....	rough
SCARCEMENT	....	projection
SCATOLOGICAL	....	obscene
SCELESTIOUS	....	evil
SCEVITY	....	unfortunate
SCHISMATIC	....	dissenter
SCHLEMIEL	....	awkward
SCIENTER	....	knowledge
SCIOLISTIC	....	superficial
SCION	....	descendant
SCLEROUS	....	hardened
SCOPULA	....	broom
SCOTOMA	....	blind-spot
SCRIVENER	....	writer
SCROFULOUS	....	soiled
SCRUPULOUS	....	integrity
SCURRILOUS	....	abusive
SECUND	....	unilateral
SEDELOUS	....	diligent
SEDITION	....	anti-government

SEI: SIB:

SEIGNIORY	....	boss
SELCOUTH	....	unusual
SEMBLABLE	....	ostensible
SEMINAL	....	original
SENECTITUDE	....	senior
SENESCENT	....	aging
SENSIFEROUS	....	sensitive
SENTENTIA	....	maxim
SENTENTIOUS	....	self-righteous
SENTIENT	....	aware
SEPTENTRIONAL	....	northern
SEQUESTRATION	....	separated
SERACS	....	ice-tower
SESQUIPEDALIAN	....	wordy
SETACEOUS	....	bristled
SEVERAL	....	separate
SEXAGESIMAL	....	sixtieth
SHIBBLETH	....	slogan
SIBILANT	....	hissing
SIBYLLINE	....	prophetic

SID: SOL:

SID		SOL
SIDEREAL	....	stary
SIGMATISM	....	mispronunciation
SIMULACRUM	....	pretense
SINCIPUT	....	forehead
SINECURIST	....	lazy
SINGULAR	....	unique
SINUOUS	....	winding
SIRENIC	....	attractive
SKELLUM	....	rascal
SLUMGULLION	....	stew
SOBRIQUET	....	nickname
SODALITY	....	society
SOIGNE	....	sophisticated
SOIREES	....	parties
SOLECISM	....	mistake
SOLECISTIC	....	ungrammatical
SOLICITOUS	....	worried
SOLIDARY	....	united
SOLIPSISM	....	egoistic
SOLITUDINARIAM	....	recluse

SOMATIC	....	physical
SOMBROUS	....	somber
SOMNAMBULISM	....	sleepwalking
SOMNOLENT	....	sleepy
SONANCE	....	sound
SOPHISTIC	....	illogical
SOPHISTRY	....	deception
SOPORIFEROUS	....	asleep
SOPORIFIC	....	sleepiness
SORORAL	....	sisterly
SOUBRETTE	....	maidservant
SOVRANLY	....	supremely
SPECIOUS	....	deceptive
SPECTRAL	....	ghostlike
SPELUNKING	....	caving
SPLENETIC	....	irritable
SPLORE	....	carousal
SPOLIATE	....	steal
SPURIOUS	....	false
STANCHION	....	pillar

STASIS	....	inertia
STENOSIS	....	narrowing
STENTORIAN	....	loud
STERTOROUS	....	loud
STILETO	....	dagger
STOCHASTIC	....	random
STOLIDITY	....	apathy
STOUR	....	battle
STROBIC	....	spinning
STULTIFY	....	foolish
STUPEFACTION	....	jerk
STYGIAN	....	gloomy
SUBALTERN	....	subordinate
SUBLIME	....	glorious
SUBLUNARY	....	terrestrial
SUBSUMED	....	included
SUBULATED	....	pointed
SUBUMBER	....	cover
SUI GENERIS	....	unique
SUPERANNUATE	....	dated

SUPEREROGATORY	....	superfluous
SUPERFLUOUS	....	unnecessary
SUPERNAL	....	heavenly
SUPERNUMERARY	....	extra
SUPPLICATE	....	plead
SUPPOSITITIOUS	....	dishonest
SUPPURATE	....	fester
SURCEASE	....	terminate
SURPLUSAGE	....	surplus
SUSTENTATION	....	keep
SUSURRATION	....	hint
SUSURRATION	....	whispering
SUSURROUS	....	whispering
SVELTE	....	urbane
SYBARITE	....	wealthy
SYCHRONOUS	....	contemporaneous
SYCOPHANTS	....	flatterer
SYLLOGISM	....	reasoning
SYMBIOSIS	....	mutualism
SYNCHRONISM	....	timetable

SYN: SYS:

SYNERGY	....	combination
SYNOPTIC	....	comprehensive
SYNTHESIS	....	combination
SYSTEMIC	....	everywhere
SYSTOLE	....	contraction

CHAPTER
T

TABESCENCE	....	diminishment
TACHYCARDIA	....	rapid-heart
TACTITURN	....	silent
TACTILE	....	tangible
TAILSMAN	....	magical
TATTERDEMALION	....	ruffian
TANKARD	....	mug
TAUROMACHY	....	bullfighting
TAUTOLOGICAL	....	repetitious
TEGUMENT	....	cover

TEMERARIOUS	....	reckless
TEMERITY	....	audacity
TEMPORIZE	....	compromise
TENDENTIOUS	....	biased
TENEBRIFIC	....	obscuring
TENEBROUS	....	dark
TEPHROSIS	....	cremation
TERATOID	....	monster
TEREBRATE	....	sting
TERGIVERSATION	....	ambiguity
TERMAGANT	....	nagger
TERMINOLOGICAL	....	technical-terms
TERTIARY	....	thirdly
TESSELLATED	....	inlaid
TETCHY	....	irritable
THAUMATURGIC	....	miraculous
THAUMATURGIST	....	magician
THESPIAN	....	actor
THEWLESS	....	weak
THOWLESS	....	listless

THR: TRA:

THRALDOM	....	servitude
THRALL	....	slavery
THRENODY	....	lament
THRIX	....	hair
THROMBOSIS	....	clot
THYMION	....	wart
TIMOROUS	....	timid
TINTINNABULATION	....	ringing
TITFER	....	hat
TITIVATE	....	adorn
TITUBATION	....	staggering
TIVITATE	....	spruce-up
TOCSIN	....	alarm
TORPID	....	sluggish
TORPOR	....	apathy
TOTEMIC	....	emblematic
TRACTABLE	....	controllable
TRADUCE	....	slander
TRADUCEMENT	....	harm
TRANSLUNARY	....	heavenly

TRANSMOGRIFY	....	transform
TRANSMUTE	....	transform
TRANSMUTATIONAL	....	conversion
TREMULOUS	....	trembling
TRENCHANT	....	effective
TRIPLICITY	....	threefold
TRISMUS	....	gnash
TRITURATE	....	crush
TROGLODYTIC	....	primitive
TRUCULENT	....	quarrelsome
TRUNCATE	....	blunted
TUBER	....	swelling
TUMESCENT	....	swollen
TUMESENCE	....	swelling
TURBID	....	muddy
TURBIDITY	....	cloudiness
TUSSIS	....	cough
TUTELARY	....	guardian
TYPHLOSIS	....	sightless

CHAPTER
U

UBEROUS	....	prolific
UBIQUITOUS	....	omnipresent
ULTRA VIRES	....	unauthorized
ULULATE	....	wail
ULULATION	....	hysterical
UNBARBED	....	shaven
UMBERMENT	....	throng
UNBRAGEOUS	....	shady
UNBOSOM	....	disclose
UNCINATED	....	hooked

UNC: UXO:

UNCTUOUS	....	insincere
UNEXPURGATED	....	unremoved
UNGUENT	....	ointment
UNREQUITED	....	unreturned
URSINE	....	bear-like
USTULATION	....	heated
USURY	....	interest
UTILITARIANISM	....	beneficial
UVULA	....	lobe
UXORIOUS	....	submissive

CHAPTER
V

VACUOUS	....	empty
VAGARY	....	impulsive
VAGINATE	....	sheathed
VAGROM	....	wandering
VAINGLORIOUS	....	perplexed
VALETUDINARIAN	....	sickly
VALIANCE	....	valor
VATICINATION	....	prediction
VELLEITY	....	wish
VELLUM	....	parchment

VENAL	....	bribable
VENALITY	....	corrupt
VENENATE	....	poison
VENERIOUS	....	lustful
VENIAL	....	pardonable
VERIDIC	....	truthful
VERISIMILITUDE	....	truth
VERMICULATE	....	dishonest
VERNAL	....	spring
VERTIGINOUS	....	whirling
VESICATE	....	blister
VESTMENT	....	robe
VICINAL	....	near
VICISSITUDE	....	changeable
VIDUITY	....	widowhood
VIGNERON	....	winegrower
VILIPEND	....	revile
VIRAGO	....	shrew
VIRULIFEROUS	....	infectious
VISCEROTONIC	....	happy-go-lucky

VIS: VUL:

VISCID	....	sticky
VITIATE	....	nullify
VITRIOLIC	....	biting
VITUPERATION	....	criticism
VOCIFEROUS	....	outcry
VOLUPTUARY	....	sensual
VORTIGINOUS	....	whirling
VOTARIES	....	follower
VOUCHSAFE	....	condescend
VULPINE	....	crafty

CHAPTER
W

WAGGERY	....	trickery
WAGGISH	....	funny
WAMBLE	....	unsteady
WASPISH	....	irritable
WASSAIL	....	toast
WASTAGE	....	erosion
WELTER	....	jumble
WIDDERSHINS	....	counterclockwise
WONTED	....	ordinary
WRAITH	....	ghost

CHAPTER
X

XANTHIC	....	yellow
XANTHIPPE	....	shrew
XAXIS	....	axis
XEBEC	....	sailing-ship
XENOPHOBIA	....	anti-foreign
XENOPHILE	....	foreign-lover
XENOPHOBE	....	foreign-hater
XERIC	....	dry
XYLOID	....	wood-like
XYLOSE	....	sugar

CHAPTER
Y

YAMMER	....	mummur
YAXIS	....	axis
YEGG	....	robber
YELK	....	yoke
YERK	....	vigorously
YEUKY	....	itchy
YOKEMATE	....	workmate
YOUNKER	....	gentlemen
YUAN	....	Chinese-dollar
YURT	....	tent

CHAPTER
Z

ZABERNISM	....	abuse-of-power
ZENANA	....	harem
ZEPHYR	....	breeze
ZOILIST	....	faultfinder
ZOOID	....	animal-like
ZOOMORPHIC	....	animal-like
ZUCCHETTO	....	skull cap
ZYME	....	fermenting
ZYMURGY	....	fermentation

BOOK II

common words to COMPLEX WORDS

chapter
a

absorbent	....	BIBULOUS
absorption	....	OSMOSIS
abuse-of-power	....	ZABERNISM
abusive	....	SCURRILOUS
accessible	....	PERVIOUS
accessory	....	ACCOUTREMENT
accessory	....	ANCILLA
accidental	....	ADVENTITIOUS
accompanying	....	APPURTENANT
accompanying	....	CONCOMITANT

accomplishable	....	FACILE
accord	....	CONSONANCE
acquit	....	EXCULPATE
across	....	ATHWART
actor	....	THESPIAN
adjacent	....	JUXTAPOSED
adjoining	....	COUNTERMINOUS
adjunct	....	APPURTENANCE
adjure	....	CONJURE
admonish	....	IMPUGNED
adoring	....	ANACREONTIC
adorn	....	RACINAGE
adorn	....	TITIVATE
advance	....	ANABASIS
advanced	....	PRECOSIOUS
advocate	....	PARACLETE
afraid	....	AFFRIGHTED
after-dinner	....	POSTPRANDIAL
afterlife	....	ESCHATOLOGY
aging	....	SENESCENT

agitated	....	FLURRIED
agrarian	....	GEOPONIC
agreeable	....	AMENITY
agreeable	....	COMPLAISANT
agreeing	....	CONSENTANEOUS
airy	....	ETHEREAL
alacrity	....	LEGERITY
alarm	....	TOCSIN
alcoholic	....	DIPSOMANIAC
aliases	....	POLYONYMOUS
all-powerful	....	CUNCTIPOTENT
alter	....	CAPONIZE
ambiguity	....	TERGIVERSATION
ambush	....	AMBUSCADE
amorous	....	AMATIVE
analogous	....	ANALOG
analyze	....	ANATOMIZE
ancestor	....	PROGENITOR
ancient	....	ANTEDILUVIAN
anesthetic	....	ANODYNE

animal-like	....	ZOOMORPHIC
animal-like	....	ZOOID
annoying	....	PESTIFEROUS
annul	....	OBROGATION
ant	....	PISMIRE
anticipate	....	PREVENIENT
anticipate	....	PROLEPIC
anti-foreign	....	XENOPHOBIA
anti-government	....	INCIVISM
anti-government	....	SEDITION
apart	....	ABSTRACT
apart	....	NOETIC
apathy	....	STOLIDITY
apathy	....	TORPOR
ape	....	ANTHROPOID
appease	....	PROPITIATE
appendages	....	ADNEXA
appointment	....	ASSIGNATION
appropriate	....	ARROGATE
approve	....	HOMOLOGATE

arg: aut:

argumentative	....	ERISTIC
aristocracy	....	PATRICIATE
armchair	....	FAUTEUIL
arousing	....	EROGENOUS
artificial	....	ERSATZ
artificial	....	FACTITIOUS
ascending	....	ACLIVITY
asexual	....	AGAMOGENESIS
asleep	....	SOPORIFEROUS
assail	....	OPPUGN
assistance	....	CONCERTATION
assume	....	POSIT
atone	....	EXPIATE
attractive	....	NUBILE
attractive	....	PULCHRITUDINOUS
attractive	....	SIRENIC
attribute	....	ASCRIPTION
audacity	....	TEMERITY
audience	....	ECCLESIA
authority	....	FACULTATIVE

authority	....	HEGEMONY
autopsy	....	NECROPSY
avert	....	FORFEND
awakening	....	ENTELECHY
awakening	....	EPIPHANY
awakening	....	INCIPIENT
aware	....	SENTIENT
awkward	....	MALADROIT
awkward	....	SCHLEMIEL
axis	....	XAXIS
axis	....	YAXIS
azure	....	CERULEAN

■ |

chapter
b

backward	....	RETROGRADE
bacterium	....	BACILLUS
bacterium	....	PATHOGEN
bad	....	NEFARIOUS
balanced	....	EQUIPONDERANT
ballet-duet	....	ADAGIO
banter	....	PERSIFLAGE
barge	....	BUCENTAUR
barter	....	NIFFER
bat	....	NOCTULE

bat: ben:

bats	....	REREMICE
battle	....	STOUR
beaded	....	MONILIFORM
beaming	....	EFFULGENT
beards-study of	....	POGONOLOGY
bear-like	....	URSINE
beating	....	BASTINADO
beauty	....	PULCHRITUDE
beg	....	IMPORTUNE
beggar	....	MENDICANT
beginner	....	ABECEDARIAN
beginning	....	EXORDIUM
beginnings	....	INCUNABULA
behavior	....	COMPORTMENT
belch	....	ERUCT
believable	....	COLORABLE
belt	....	CINCTURE
bend	....	GENUFLECT
bend	....	RETORTION
beneficial	....	SALUTARY

ben:

ble:

beneficial	....	UTILITARIANISM
beside	....	LIMITROPHE
bewitch	....	ENSORCEL
biased	....	TENDENTIOUS
billion	....	MILLIARD
birthing	....	ACCOUCHEMENT
birthing	....	NASCENT
bisexual	....	ANDROGYNOUS
biting	....	ACIDULOUS
biting	....	MORDANT
biting	....	MORDOCIOUS
biting	....	VITRIOLIC
bitter	....	ACRID
blackhead	....	COMEDO
blame	....	INCULPATE
blasphemy	....	PROFANATION
bleaching	....	DEALBATION
blemish	....	MACULATE
blend	....	CONFLATION
blessing	....	BENISON

blind-spot	....	SCOTOMA
blindess	....	ABLEPSIA
blink	....	NICTITATE
bliss	....	BEATIFIC
blissful	....	ELYSIAN
blister	....	VESICATE
blood-relation	....	CONSANGUINITY
bloody	....	SANGUINARY
blow-out	....	MEPHITIS
blue	....	AERUGINOUS
blunt	....	OBTUSE
blunted	....	TRUNCATE
blurred	....	HALATION
boasting	....	GASCONADING
boasting	....	JACTATION
boil	....	DEFFERVESCENCE
bold	....	AUDACIOUS
bold	....	MALAPERT
boldness	....	EFFRONTUOUS
bombastic	....	GRANDILOQUENCE

bom: ## bri:

bombastic	....	MAGNILOQUENT
book-collector	....	BIBLIOPHILE
book-seller	....	BIBLIOPOLE
boorish	....	CHURLISH
boorish	....	LOUTISH
boredom	....	ENNUI
boring	....	OPEROSENESS
boorish	....	LOUTISH
borrow	....	CADGE
boss	....	SEIGNIORY
bountiful	....	MUNIFICENT
boxer	....	PUGILIST
brag	....	RODOMONTADE
braggart	....	FANFARON
breeze	....	ZEPHYR
bribable	....	VENAL
bribe	....	GRATULANCE
brief	....	CADUCOUS
bright	....	CORUSCATION
bright	....	LAMBENT

bri: but:

brilliance	....	EFFULGENCE
bristled	....	SETACEOUS
broom	....	SCOPULA
bruise	....	ECCHYMOSIS
bubbles	....	EBULLITION
bullfighting	....	TAUROMACHY
burden	....	ENCUMBRANCE
burn	....	AMBUSTION
burn	....	DEFLAGRATE
burning	....	PYROTIC
burp	....	ERUCTATE
bus	....	JITNEY
busybody	....	QUIDNUNC
buttocks	....	FUNDAMENT
buttocks	....	HEINIE

chapter
c

callous	....	INDURATE
calm	....	ATARACTIC
calm	....	HALCYON
cancer	....	CARCINOMA
cannibalism	....	ANTHROPOPHAGY
car	....	FLIVER
carousal	....	SPLORE
cashless	....	ILLIQUID
casket	....	RELIQUARY
catharsis	....	ABRECTION

cat: cha:

cathouse	....	BAGNIO
cat-lover	....	AELUROPHILE
cause	....	ETIOLOGY
caution	....	CHARINESS
cautious	....	CLARY
caving	....	SPELUNKING
cavity	....	ALVEOLUS
challenge	....	OBACERATE
chameleon	....	PROTEAN
champion	....	KEMP
change	....	DEDIFFERENTICTION
changeable	....	MUTABLE
changeable	....	VICISSITUDE
chanting	....	INCANTATION
chaperone	....	DUENNA
charing	....	INTUMESCENT
charitable	....	ELEEMOSYNARY
charm	....	AMULET
chastity	....	CONTINENCE
chat	....	CONFABULATE

chatter	....	PALAVER
chatter	....	PRATE
chauvinism	....	JINGOISM
cheat	....	COZEN
cheek	....	BUCCAL
cheerful	....	ALACRITY
cheerful	....	SANGUINE
cheesy	....	CASEOUS
chew	....	MASTICATE
chewing	....	MACHONNEMENT
childbirth	....	PARTURITION
childish	....	PUERILE
childishness	....	PUERLISM
children	....	PROGENY
chilly	....	GELID
Chinese-dollar	....	YUAN
chord	....	ARPEGGIO
circle-like	....	CIRCUMFERENTIALLY
cleanse	....	BOWDLERIZE
clear	....	LIMPID

cliff	....	ESCARPMENT
clockwise	....	DEASIL
closing	....	OBTURATION
clot	....	THROMBOSIS
cloth	....	ACCOUTER
clothing	....	HABILIMENT
cloud	....	NIMBUS
cloudiness	....	TURBIDITY
coercion	....	PERFORCE
coffin	....	SARCOPHAGUS
coin-like	....	NUMMULAR
coldness	....	ALGIDITY
collar	....	COLLET
collector	....	ANTIQUARIAN
combination	....	SYNTHESIS
combination	....	SYNERGY
comic	....	HARLEQUIN
command	....	MANDAMUS
commonplace	....	PEDESTRIAN
communicative	....	DEIPNOSOPHIST

com: con:

com		con
compensate	....	COUNTERVAIL
complaining	....	CARPING
complaining	....	KVETCHY
compliment	....	PRECONIZE
composite	....	MONTAGE
comprehensive	....	SYNOPTIC
compromise	....	TEMPORIZE
conceal	....	PALLIATE
concise	....	BRACHYLOGY
concise	....	EPIGRAMMATIC
conclusion	....	PERORATION
concubine	....	ODALISQUE
concur	....	BAITHE
condescend	....	VOUCHSAFE
conductor	....	IMPRESARIO
confess	....	INTROMIT
confidential	....	ESOTERIC
confirmation	....	HOMOLOGATION
confiscate	....	ESCHEAT
conforming	....	CANONICAL

confuse	....	BEMUSE
confuse	....	OBFUSCATE
confused	....	FLUMMOXED
confused	....	GALIMATIAS
confused	....	OBNUBILATION
confusing	....	ABSTRUSE
confusing	....	ENIGMA
confusing	....	OBSCURANTISM
confusing	....	RECONDITE
considering	....	LISTENABLE
constipated	....	OBSTIPATED
constrictive	....	ASTRINGENT
contaminate	....	ADULTERATE
contemporaneous	....	SYCHRONOUS
contemporaneous	....	COEVAL
contemporary	....	MODERNITY
contiguous	....	CONTERMINOUS
contraction	....	SYSTOLE
contributory	....	ADJUVANT
controllable	....	TRACTABLE

conversation	....	INTERLOCUTION
conversion	....	TRANSMUTATIONAL
convincing	....	COGENT
copy	....	APOGRAPH
copying	....	MIMETIC
cordiality	....	RAPPROCHEMENT
corrupt	....	VENALITY
cotton-cloth	....	MOLLETON
cough	....	TUSSIS
counterclockwise	....	WIDDERSHINS
courageous	....	OULTREPREU
course	....	SALEBROSITY
courteous	....	COMITY
courtly	....	AULIC
cover	....	SUBUMBER
cover	....	TEGUMENT
covering	....	PANOPLY
covetous	....	PLEONEXIA
coward	....	CRAVEN
coward	....	POLTROUN

cow: cul:

cowardly	....	PUSILLANIMOUS
cowboyish	....	BUBULCITATA
crafty	....	VULPINE
crash	....	NAUFRAGATE
crater	....	CALDERA
cremation	....	TEPHROSIS
crevices	....	INTERSTICES
criminal	....	MALFACTOR
critical	....	CENSORIOUS
criticism	....	VITUPERATION
criticism	....	DIATRIBE
criticize	....	ABRADE
criticize	....	CASTIGATE
criticize	....	EXCORIATE
crossing	....	DECUSSATE
crucial	....	CLIMACTERIC
crude	....	AGRESTIC
cruel	....	DISPITEOUS
crush	....	TRITURATE
culmination	....	APOGEE

cul: ## cus:

culmination	....	PERIGEE
cupid	....	AMORETTO
cure-all	....	PANACEA
curse	....	ANATHEMA
curse	....	IMPRECATION
curse	....	MALEDICTION
curse	....	PISHOGUE
curt	....	LACONIC
curved	....	AQUILINE
customary	....	CONSUETUDINARY

chapter
d

dagger	....	STILETO
daily	....	DIURNAL
damp	....	AESCENT
dance	....	DANDLE
dancing	....	SALTANT
dangerous	....	PARLOUS
dark	....	APHOTIC
dark	....	CALIGINOUS
dark	....	TENEBROUS
darken	....	OBNUBILATE

dated	....	SUPERANNUATE
dead	....	NECROTIC
debate	....	DIALECTIC
debate	....	DISPUTATION
debative	....	POLEMICAL
deceit	....	INGANNATION
deception	....	SOPHISTRY
deceptive	....	DELUSIVE
deceptive	....	SPECIOUS
decomposing	....	SARCOLYTIC
defense	....	MUNIMENT
definition	....	CIRCUMSCRIPTION
degeneration	....	DEVOLUTION
delay	....	LACHES
delicious	....	SAPID
deliverance	....	RIDDANCE
denial	....	RECUSANCY
dense	....	IMPORUS
denunciation	....	FULMINATE
deny	....	GAINSAY

depressed	....	ABJECT
deprive	....	EVISCERATE
descendant	....	SCION
deserved	....	MERITOCRACY
desiring	....	ORECTIC
desk	....	ESCRITOIRE
destroy	....	EXTIRPATE
destroy	....	INTERDICT
destructive	....	PERNICIOUS
detestable	....	EXECRATIVE
detested	....	EXECTRATED
deviating	....	AWRY
dialect	....	IDIOM
dictionary	....	LEXICON
different	....	ANTIPHRASTIC
digest	....	CONSPECTUS
digestible	....	ESCULENT
digression	....	DIVAGATION
diligent	....	ASSIDUOUS
diligent	....	SEDELOUS

dim: dis:

dim:		dis:
diminish	....	TABESCENCE
dimness	....	AMPLYOPIA
diplomat	....	PLENIPOTENTIARY
direct	....	ACULEATE
disagreeable	....	CURMUDGEON
disappearance	....	LYSIS
disapproval	....	DISAPPROBATION
disapprove	....	REDARQUE
disarray	....	DISHABILLE
disclose	....	UNBOSOM
discontinue	....	ROROGUE
discord	....	DISSONANCE
disdain	....	DYSOLISTIC
disease	....	IATROGENIC
diseased	....	PANDEMIC
diseased	....	PATHOGENIC
disgrace	....	OBLOQUY
disgraceful	....	OPPROBRIUM
disgusting	....	FULSOME
disgustingly	....	FURCIFEROUS

dis: ## dis:

dishonest	....	MENDACIOUS
dishonest	....	SUPPOSITITIOUS
dishonest	....	VERMICULATE
dishonesty	....	CASUISTRY
dislike	....	ANTIPATHY
dislocation	....	LUXATION
disloyalty	....	APOSTASY
dismiss	....	CASHIER
disobedient	....	CONTUMACIOUS
disorder	....	ENTROPY
disparagement	....	EPITHET
disparaging	....	PEJORATIVE
disputation	....	CONFUTATION
dispute	....	ELENCHUS
dispute	....	CONTESTATION
disputing	....	CHOPLOGIC
disregard	....	IMPUDENCE
dissent	....	DISIDENCE
dissenter	....	SCHISMATIC
distinct	....	DISPARATE

distorted	....	ANAMORPHOSIS
distribution	....	REPARTITION
disuse	....	DESUETUDE
diversity	....	MUTIFARIOUSNESS
divide	....	BATTRICE
divide	....	BIFURCATE
divination	....	RHABDOMANTIST
divine	....	NUMINOUS
division	....	CANTON
division	....	DICHOTOMY
division	....	PARTITION
dominant	....	PREPONDERANT
dote	....	DRIVEL
doubtless	....	PROVENLY
downward	....	DECLIVITY
drastic	....	PROCRUSTEAN
draw	....	LIMNED
dreaded	....	REDOUBTABLE
dreary	....	DRIEGH
dried	....	DESICCATE

dri: dyi:

drinking	....	BRANNIGAN
drug-addiction	....	NARCOMANIA
drunkard	....	INTEMPERANCE
drunken	....	BACCHANALIAN
dry	....	XERIC
dull	....	PROSAIC
dullness	....	HEBETUDE
dumb	....	CRASSITUDE
dumping	....	QUENNELLE
dying	....	MORIBUND

chapter
e

earwax	....	CERUMEN
ease	....	PALLIATIVE
eatable	....	COMESTIBLE
edible	....	ESCLUENT
edit	....	EMEND
edit	....	REDACT
edit	....	EXPERGATE
education	....	HYPNOPEDIA
effective	....	EFFLICACIOUS
effective	....	REDOUND

eff: emp:

effective	....	TRENCHANT
effeminate	....	EPICENE
effluence	....	EXTRAVASATE
eggplant-color	....	AUBERGINE
egoistic	....	SOLIPSISM
election	....	COOPTION
electric	....	GALVANIC
elementary	....	RUDIMENTARY
eliminate	....	ENCOPRESIS
eloquent	....	EUPHUISTIC
emancipation	....	MANUMISSION
embankment	....	REVETMENTS
embarrassing	....	CONTUMELIOUS
embarrassment	....	CONTRATEMPS
embarrassment	....	DISCOMFITURE
embezzlement	....	DEFALCATION
embezzlement	....	PECULATION
emblematic	....	TOTEMIC
empty	....	INANE
empty	....	VACUOUS

enclose	....	INTUSSUSCEPT
enclose	....	INVAGINATE
encourage	....	INSPIRIT
encouraging	....	HORTATIVE
encumbrance	....	FARDEL
end	....	CLOTURE
ending	....	DECRESCENT
endowment	....	DOTATION
enhancement	....	LIONIZATION
enlarge	....	AUGMENT
enlarged	....	ACCRESCENT
enlargement	....	ELEPHANTIASIS
entanglement	....	IMBROGLIO
entice	....	INVIGLE
environment	....	MILIEU
epigrams	....	ANTHOLOGY
equality	....	EGALITARIAN
equivalent	....	EQUIPOLLENT
erosion	....	WASTAGE
error	....	CORRIGENDUM

err:		**exp:**
errorless	....	DISABUSED
erupting	....	DISSILIENT
escape	....	ABSQUATULATE
essential	....	GRAVAMEN
eulogy	....	PANEGYRIC
evening	....	CREPUSCULE
evergreen	....	CONIFER
everlasting	....	ETERNE
everywhere	....	SYSTEMIC
evil	....	SCELESTIOUS
evil-spirit	....	CACODEMON
evildoer	....	MALEFACTOR
exaggerated	....	FUSTIAN
exaggerating	....	MYTHOMANSIA
exaggeration	....	HYPERBOLIC
excellent	....	EXIMIOUS
excited	....	DITHYRAMBIC
exhausted	....	DELASSATION
exhaustion	....	INANITION
expand	....	PROTUBERATE

exp: ext:

expert	....	COGNOSCENTE
expert	....	MAVIN
explanation	....	EXCLAMATION
explanation	....	EXEGESIS
explanatory	....	EXEGETICAL
exposed	....	PATULOUS
exposure	....	EXPOSE
externalize	....	HYPOSTATIZE
extra	....	SUPERNUMERARY
extraction	....	RENDITION
extraordinary	....	PLUPERFECT
extravagance	....	PROFLIGACY

chapter
f

fact	....	IMPIGROUS
fail	....	MISASSAY
faithless	....	PERFIDY
faker	....	MALINGERER
false	....	APOCRYPHAL
false	....	FLAMBUGINOUS
false	....	POSTICHE
false	....	SPURIOUS
falsehood	....	PARALOGISM
fare	....	FERRIAGE

far: fev:

farsighted	....	PRESBYOPIA
fasten	....	COAPTATION
fat	....	CORPULENT
fat	....	PINGUID
fat	....	PLENITUDINOUS
father	....	PATERFAMILIAS
fatigue	....	LASSITUDE
faultfinder	....	ZOILIST
faultfinding	....	CAPTIOUS
favorable	....	PROPITIOUS
fear	....	PAVOR
fearless	....	INTREPID
feces	....	EXCREMENTITIOUS
feeble	....	IMPUISSANCE
fermentation	....	ZYMURGY
fermenting	....	ZYME
fertile	....	FECUND
fertility	....	FECUNDITY
fester	....	SUPPURATE
feverless	....	AFEBRILE

fid: fli:

fidelity	....	FEALTY
figuratively	....	ALLEGORICAL
fine	....	AMERCEMENT
fireball	....	CORPOSANT
fisherman	....	PISCATOR
fit	....	PAOXYSM
flag	....	FANION
flaming	....	FLAMBEAU
flash	....	FULGURATION
flask	....	COSTREL
flatter	....	ADULATORY
flatter	....	INVEIGLE
flatterer	....	SYCOPHANTS
flattering	....	GNATHONIC
flattery	....	FLUMMERY
flatulence	....	BORBORYEM
flavor	....	SAPOR
fleeting	....	FUGACIOUS
flesh	....	SARCOUS
flippant	....	FLACETIOUS

flirt	....	COQUETTISH
floating	....	NATANT
flowery	....	FLORID
flowing	....	CIRCUMFLUENT
flowing	....	EFFLUENCE
followed	....	VOTARIES
followers	....	RETINUE
food	....	ALIMENT
food	....	PROVENDER
fool	....	GOMERAL
fool	....	HAVEREL
fool	....	NODDY
foolish	....	FATUOUS
foolish	....	STULTIFY
forehead	....	SINCIPUT
foreign	....	HETEROCHTHONOUS
foreign-hater	....	XENOPHOBE
foreign-lover	....	XENOPHILE
foreknowledge	....	PRESCIENT
foreshadowing	....	PORTENTOUS

for: fri:

forge	....	FAUXER
forgetful	....	DISTRAITE
formless	....	INCORPOREAL
fortification	....	BREASTWORK
fortification	....	REDOUBT
fossil	....	CONODONT
fossils	....	PALEONTOLOGY
foul	....	FECULENT
fourth	....	QUADRENNIAL
fox	....	REYNARD
fractional	....	ALIQUOT
fragile	....	FRANGIBLE
fragrant	....	REDOLENT
fragranced	....	MYRRHED
frantic	....	FRENETIC
fraud	....	OBREPTION
free	....	CARCELAGE
free	....	MANUMIT
frenzied	....	CORYBANTIC
friendly	....	CONVIVIAL

friendly	....	GRAGARIOUS
frigid	....	HYPERBOREAN
frugality	....	PARSIMONIOUS
fulfillment	....	EFFLORESCENCE
full	....	REPLETION
funeral-rite	....	OBSEQUY
funny	....	RISIBLE
funny	....	WAGGISH
fuss	....	POTHER
fussy	....	MORDACIOUS

chapter
g

gale	....	HENGHEN
gallery	....	CLERESTORY
gaudy	....	BEDIZEN
gaudy	....	MERETRICIOUS
generals	....	DERGE
generosity	....	LARGESSE
gentleman	....	YOUNKER
gentleness	....	LENITY
gentleness	....	MANSUETUDE
germless	....	ASEPTIC

ghastly	....	CADAVEROUS
ghost	....	WRAITH
ghost-like	....	SPECTRAL
ghostly	....	CHTHONIC
giantness	....	ACROMEGALY
glide	....	GLISSADE
gloomy	....	ATRABILIOUS
gloomy	....	SATURINE
gloomy	....	STYGIAN
glorious	....	SUBLIME
glutinous	....	POLYPHAGIA
glutton	....	CRAPULOUS
glutton	....	GOURMAND
gluttonous	....	CRAPULENCE
gluttonous	....	EDACIOUS
gluttonous	....	GULOSITOUS
gnash	....	TRISMUS
goddess	....	DIVA
god-like	....	ICON
godman	....	DEMIGOD

god: gro:

god:		gro:
gods-in-nature	....	PANTHEISM
good-looking	....	ILLECEBROUS
gourd	....	CALABASH
government	....	POLITY
grant	....	APPANAGE
grasping	....	PREHENSILE
grasping	....	PREHENSION
grassy	....	GRAMINEOUS
gratuity	....	CUMSHAN
graveyard	....	NECROPOLIS
grayish	....	CANESCENT
greed	....	CUPIDITY
greed	....	AVIDITY
greedy	....	AVARICIOUS
greedy	....	CUPIDINOUS
greedy	....	ESURIENT
groin	....	INGUINAL
group	....	COTERIE
growth	....	ACRETION
growth	....	HISTOGENSIS

gru: ## gun:

gruesome   ....   MACABRE

guardian   ....   TUTELARY

guide   ....   CICERONE

gunfire   ....   FUSILLADE

chapter
h

habitual	....	INVETERATE
hair	....	THRIX
hairless	....	ALOPECIA
hair-like	....	PHILIFORM
hair-removal	....	DEPILATE
hairsplitting	....	PILPUL
hairy	....	HIRSUTE
hairy	....	LANUGINOUS
hairy	....	PILOSE
half	....	MOIETY

hal: har:

halitosis	....	OZOSTOMIA
happiness	....	EUDEMONIA
happy	....	JOCUND
happy	....	LAETIFICANT
happy-go-lucky	....	VISCEROTONIC
hard	....	ADAMANTINE
hard	....	CEMENTITIOUS
harden	....	OSSIFY
hardened	....	INDURATED
hardened	....	SCLEROUS
hardwood	....	DECIDUOUS
harem	....	ZENANA
harm	....	TRADUCEMENT
harmful	....	BALEFUL
harmful	....	MALEFIC
harmful	....	NOCUOUS
harmless	....	INNOCUOUS
harmony	....	CONCINNITY
harsh	....	CACOPHONY
harshness	....	ACRIMONY

hastening	....	FESTINATE
hat	....	TITFER
hater	....	MISANDROUS
hater	....	MISANTHROPIC
hatred	....	ODIUM
haughtiness	....	HAUTEUR
headband	....	DIADEM
healing	....	SANATIVE
hearing	....	AUSCULTATION
heated	....	USTULATION
heating	....	CALEFACIENT
heaven	....	EMPYREAN
heavenly	....	SUPERNAL
heavenly	....	TRANSLUNARY
hell	....	PERDITION
henchman	....	MYRMIDON
hermit	....	ANCHORITE
hermit	....	EREMITE
hierarchy	....	GERARCHY
hint	....	SUSURRATION

his: **hum:**

hissing	....	SIBILANT
historian	....	ANNALIST
hoax	....	PUTON
hold	....	INTELLECTION
hold-up	....	DEMURRAGE
homesickness	....	NOSTOMANIA
homosexuality	....	DIONISM
homosexuality	....	HOMOEROTOCISM
honest	....	PROBITY
hooked	....	UNCINATED
horrible	....	EGREGIOUS
horse-drawn	....	EQUIPAGE
horsemanship	....	MANÈGE
hostile	....	OPPUNGNANT
hue	....	MAGNOLIOUS
hue	....	MOLIMINOUS
huge	....	BROBDINGNAGIAN
huge	....	CYCLOPEAN
hum	....	BOMBINATE
humanistic	....	ANTHROPOMORPHIC

hyp: hys:

hypnotism   ....   BRAIDISM

hysterical   ....   ULULATION

chapter
i

ice-tower	....	SERACS
ideal	....	APOTHEOSIS
identical	....	ISOMORPHIC
idle	....	OTIOSE
idol	....	MAUMET
idolatry	....	IMPIOUS
ignorance	....	NESCIENCE
ill-health	....	CACHEXIA
illiterate	....	ALEXIA
illogical	....	SOPHISTIC

illusion	....	CHIMERA
imaginary	....	CHIMERICAL
imaginary	....	EIDOLON
imitation	....	PARODY
immortality	....	ATHANASIA
impartitionable	....	INDISCERPTIBLE
impassive	....	PHLEGMATIC
imperturbable	....	SANGFROID
implore	....	ADJURE
impractical	....	QUIXOTIC
improve	....	AMELIORATE
improvements	....	MALIORATIONS
impulsive	....	CAPRICIOUS
impulsive	....	MEGRIM
impulsive	....	VAGARY
inactive	....	HUDERON
inactive	....	PERCUNCTORILY
inappropriate	....	MALAPROPISMS
inbreeding	....	HOMOGAMY
inchronological	....	ANACHRONISM

included	....	SUBSUMED
inclusion	....	IRREDENTISM
incomplete	....	INCHOATE
incomprehension	....	APHASIA
incongruous	....	OXYMORON
inconsistent	....	INCONSONANT
inconvenient	....	INCOMMODIOUS
incurable	....	IMMEDICABLE
independence	....	AUTARKY
independently	....	AUTOGENOUS
independently	....	AUTOLOGOUS
independently	....	ENDOGENOUS
indigestion	....	DYSPEPTIC
indirectness	....	OBIQUITY
indistinguishable	....	FUNGIBLE
inertia	....	STASIS
inexcusable	....	ASININITIES
infatuated	....	INSENSATE
infectious	....	VIRULIFEROUS
inference	....	RATIOCINATION

inf: int:

inferior	....	DRECK
inferior	....	EPIGONE
inflexible	....	OBDURATE
inheritance	....	HEREDITAMENT
inheritance	....	PATRIMONY
initiator	....	REAGENT
inlaid	....	TESSELLATED
insatiable	....	INSATIATE
insert	....	INTERCALATE
insert	....	INTERPOLATE
insight	....	APERCUS
insincere	....	DISINGENUOUS
insincere	....	UNCTUOUS
insincerity	....	CANT
inspired	....	ORACULAR
instruction	....	MANUDUCTION
insulting	....	INVECTIVE
insulting	....	RIPOSTE
integration	....	CONCATENATION
integrity	....	SCRUPULOUS

intellect	....	PUNDIT
interest	....	USURY
interpretation	....	HERMENEUTICS
intersection	....	QUATERVOIS
intimate	....	ADUMBRATE
introductory	....	PROLEGOMENON
invective	....	PHILIPPIC
inward	....	CENTRIPETAL
iridescent	....	OPALESCENT
irrefutable	....	APODICTIC
irrefutable	....	IRREFRAGABLE
irregularity	....	ANOMALY
irresistible	....	INELUCTABLE
irritable	....	CHOLERIC
irritable	....	QUERULOUS
irritable	....	RASPISH
irritable	....	SPLENETIC
irritable	....	TETCHY
irritable	....	WASPISH
irritating	....	REBARBATIVE

iso: iti:

isolate   ....   ENISLE

itchy   ....   YEUKY

itinerant   ....   PERIPATETIC

chapter
j

jaunty	....	RAKISH
jerk	....	STUPEFACTION
jerky	....	SACCADE
jest	....	RAILLERY
joining	....	ANASTOMOSIS
joining	....	CHAMPERTOUS
joining	....	INOSCULATE
joint	....	PARCENARY
joker	....	FARCEUR
journey	....	PEREGRINATION
jumble	....	WELTER

chapter
k

keep	....	SUSTENTATION
kill	....	INTERNECINE
kin	....	COGNATE
kind	....	BENIGNANT
kingpin	....	KINGBOLT
kiss	....	OSCULATION
klutz	....	LOUT
knife	....	KNOUT
knife	....	KWAIKEN
knot	....	COCKADE
knowledge	....	SCIENTER

chapter
l

laborious	....	OPEROSE
lament	....	THRENODY
last	....	PERDURE
laugh	....	CACHINNATE
laugh	....	FLEER
lavish	....	PROFUSE
lawbook	....	CUSTUMAL
laxative	....	APERIENT
lazy	....	FAINEANT
lazy	....	INDOLENT
lazy	....	SINECURIST

leader	....	SACHEM
leaderless	....	INTERREGNUM
lean	....	PROCUMBENT
left	....	LARBOARD
legal	....	CONQEABLE
lesbianism	....	SAPPHISM
letters	....	EPISTOLARY
levels	....	ECHELONS
lewd	....	LICENTIOUSNESS
lie	....	CANARD
lie	....	MENTITION
light-avoidance	....	PHOTOPHOBIC
lighthearted	....	INSOUCIANT
lightless	....	FUSCOUS
lightless	....	OPAQUE
limits	....	PURLIEUS
limp	....	FLACCID
limping	....	CLAUDICATION
link	....	CATENATE
link	....	NEXUS

lis: lul:

listless	....	LANGUOROUS
listless	....	THOWLESS
literary	....	ROGATION
litigious	....	BARRATRY
loan	....	IMPREST
loaned	....	MUTUATITIAL
lobe	....	UVULA
local	....	INSULAR
localized	....	ENDEMIC
logical	....	DIALECTIC
longevity	....	MACROBIOSIS
lordly	....	IMPERIOUS
loud	....	PLANGENT
loud	....	STENTORIAN
loud	....	STERTOROUS
lover	....	INAMORATA
low-light	....	CREPUSCULAR
loyal	....	LIEGE
luck	....	ALEATORIC
lullaby	....	BERCEUSE

lum: lyi:

luminous	....	REFULGENT
lustful	....	HIRCINE
lustful	....	ITHYPALLIC
lustful	....	LASCIVIOUS
lustful	....	LIBIDINOUS
lustful	....	SALACIOUS
lustful	....	VENERIOUS
lying	....	PERJURIOUS

chapter
m

magic	....	GRAMARYE
magical	....	HERMETIC
magical	....	TAILSMAN
magician	....	THAUMATURGIST
maidservant	....	SOUBRETTE
malaria	....	PALUDISM
malformation	....	DYAGENESIS
malicious	....	MALEVOLENT
manly	....	PRIAPIC
manure	....	MUCK

man: **mer:**

many-stages	....	POLYMORPHOUS
mapper	....	CARTOGRAPHER
marital	....	CONNUBIAL
martial	....	ALARUMS
matchless	....	INIMITABLE
maxim	....	SENTENTIA
meager	....	EXIGUOUS
meal	....	REPAST
meandering	....	EXCURSIVE
meandering	....	PERIPHRASTIC
meat-eater	....	CARNIVOROUS
mechanical	....	AUTOMATON
melodic	....	CANROUS
melodiously	....	DULCETLY
melt	....	DELIQUESCE
memorial	....	CAIRN
memory	....	EIDETIC
memory	....	MNEMONIC
mercenary	....	CONDOTTIERE
merge	....	AMALGAMATION

merited	....	CONDIGN
merry	....	BLITHE
middleclass	....	BOURGEOIS
midget	....	HOMUNCULUS
mimic	....	ECHOPRAXIA
mind-reader	....	CRYPTESTHESIA
miraculous	....	THAUMATURGIC
mispronunciation	....	SIGMATISM
misspeak	....	MISAVER
mistake	....	PECCABLE
mistake	....	SOLECISM
misunderstanding	....	IMPERCIPIENT
misunderstanding	....	MALENTENDU
mixed	....	ECLECTIC
mixed	....	HETEROGENEOUS
mixture	....	MELANGE
mob-rule	....	OCHLOCRACY
model	....	PARAGON
moderation	....	ABSTERMIOUS
money	....	FIVER

mon:		mum:
monster	....	TERATOID
moral	....	IMPUTRESCIBLE
moral	....	RECTITUDINOUS
morality	....	DEONTOLOGY
more	....	ADSCITITIOUS
morning	....	MATINAL
motion	....	KINESIS
motion	....	KINETIC
motivation	....	AFFLATUS
mournful	....	DOLOROUS
mournful	....	ELEGICAL
mournful	....	FUNEREAL
mournful	....	LUGUBRIOUS
mouth	....	EMBOUCHURE
move	....	DECAMP
muddy	....	TURBID
mug	....	TANKARD
multi-colored	....	PIED
multilingual	....	POLYGOT
mummur	....	YAMMER

mus: ## mys:

muscular	....	KINAESTHETIC
mushroom	....	CHAMPIGNON
music	....	CANICAL
musky	....	MOSCHATE
musty	....	FROWSTY
mute	....	OBMUTESCENCE
mutualism	....	SYMBIOSIS
mutuality	....	RECIPROCITY
mysterious	....	ARCANE
mysterious	....	INSCRUTABLE
mystical	....	ANAGOGIC
mysticism	....	GNOSIS

chapter
n

nagger	....	TERMAGANT
nagging	....	GROUSING
name	....	APPELLATION
name	....	MONIKER
narrowing	....	STENOSIS
native	....	AUTOCHTHONOUS
native	....	INDIGENOUS
natural	....	FERAL
near	....	VICINAL
neckline	....	DECOLLETAGE

nee: nov:

needle-like	....	ACEROSE
needle-like	....	ACICULAR
neglectful	....	POCOCURANTISH
nerve	....	EFFRONTERY
nervousness	....	DYSPHORIA
netlike	....	RETICULATED
new	....	NEOTERIC
next-to-last	....	PENULTIMATE
niches	....	COLUMBARIUM
nickname	....	SOBRIQUET
nightmare	....	INCUBUS
nimble	....	LISSOME
nodding	....	NUTATION
nonmetal	....	METALLOID
non-remembrance	....	OBLIVESCENCE
northern	....	SEPTENTRIONAL
nose	....	PROBOSCIS
noticeable	....	SALIENT
nourishing	....	ALIMENTARY
novice	....	POSTULANT

nuc: ## nun:

nuclei   ....   KARYOGAMY

nullify   ....   VITIATE

number   ....   COEFFICIENT

number   ....   PAGINATE

numbness   ....   ORDERMITION

nun   ....   CLOISTRESS

chapter
o

obesity	....	ADIPOSITY
object	....	EXPOSTULATE
object	....	REMONSTRATE
objection	....	EXPOSTULATION
obligation	....	OBSTRICTION
obnoxious	....	INVIDIOUS
obscene	....	SCATOLOGICAL
obscenities	....	COPROLALIA
obscuring	....	TENEBRIFIC
observation	....	INVIGILATION

obs		ord
obstinance	....	INTRACTABILITY
oceanic	....	PELAGIC
offering	....	OBLATION
official	....	MANDARIN
oil-receptive	....	OLEOPHILIC
oil-repellant	....	OLEOPHOBIC
oily	....	LUBRICIOUS
oily	....	OLEAGINOUS
ointment	....	UNGUENT
omnipresent	....	UBIQUITOUS
one-fourth	....	QUARTERN
oniony	....	ALLIACEOUS
opening	....	APERTURE
opening	....	ORIFICE
oppose	....	REPUGN
opposite	....	ANTITHESIS
opposition	....	RENITANCY
ordinary	....	BANAL
ordinary	....	BANAUSIC
ordinary	....	WONTED

ordinary	....	QUOTIDIAN
original	....	ARCHETYPAL
original	....	ARCHETYPE
original	....	PRIMORDIAL
original	....	SEMINAL
ornate	....	BAROQUE
ostensible	....	SEMBLABLE
outcry	....	VOCIFEROUS
outline	....	LINEAMENT
overweight	....	ABDOMINOUS

chapter
p

pacify	....	MOLLIFY
pairs	....	BINATE
parchment	....	VELLUM
pardon	....	IGNOSLENCY
pardonable	....	VENIAL
parent-like	....	ATAVISTIC
parties	....	SOIREES
partitionable	....	DISCERPTIBLE
passage	....	FISTULA
passionate	....	EPITHYMY

pat: phi:

pat:		phi:
patience	....	LONGANIMITY
pattern	....	PARADIGM
peaceful	....	IRENIC
peculiarity	....	IDIOSYNCRATIC
peerless	....	NONPAREIL
penmanship	....	CHIROGRAPHY
perceptive	....	SAGACIOUS
perfection	....	ANALITY
perforated	....	CRIBRIFORM
performances	....	REPERTOIRE
performers	....	ENSEMBLE
perfume	....	OLIBANUM
perhaps	....	PERADVENTURE
perhaps	....	PERCHANCE
perjured	....	MAINSWORN
perjury	....	ABJURATION
perplexed	....	NONPLUSSED
perplexed	....	VAINGLORIOUS
pertinent	....	APPOSITE
philosophical	....	METAPHYSICAL

phy: ple:

physical	....	SOMATIC
pieces	....	DETRITUS
pierced	....	FENESTRATED
pigeon	....	CUSHAT
piggish	....	PORCINE
pile	....	CONGERIES
pillar	....	STANCHION
pipe	....	CALUMET
pirate	....	CORSAIR
pity	....	PATHOS
place-together	....	COLLOCATE
plain	....	ESPLANADE
playful	....	ESPIEGLE
plead	....	OBSECRATE
plead	....	SUPPLICATE
pleasant	....	FELICITOUS
pleasing	....	PERAMENE
pleasurable	....	EPICUREAN
pleasurable	....	HEDONISTIC
pleasure	....	APOLAUSTIC

ple: **por:**

pleasure	....	DELECTATION
pledge	....	HYPOTHECATE
pledge	....	RECOGNIZANCE
plot	....	MACHINATION
plotters	....	CABAL
plunder	....	DERRECLATIONS
plunder	....	REIVE
poem	....	ELEGY
poet	....	POETASTER
pointed	....	APICULATE
pointed	....	SUBULATED
poison	....	VENENATE
poisonous	....	MEPHITIC
poisonous	....	MEPHITIE
poisonous	....	MIASMIC
polished	....	LEGGIADROUS
polished	....	LEVIGATED
ponder	....	RUMINATE
poor	....	PENURY
porous	....	PERMEABLE

pos: ## pre:

postpone	....	CUNCTATION
pour	....	AFFUSION
powderize	....	LEVIGATE
powerless	....	INERT
powerless	....	NUGATORY
power-sharing	....	COLLEGIALITY
practical-politics	....	REALPOLITIK
praise	....	ENCOMIUMS
praise	....	PAEAN
praised	....	FETTED
praising	....	PLAUSIVE
prayer	....	DEESIS
prayer	....	ORISON
precipitating	....	PLUVIOUS
predict	....	PRESAGE
prediction	....	VATICINATION
prehistoric	....	DOLMEN
prejudice	....	PREPOSSION
preliminary	....	PREFATORY
pretender	....	MOUNTEBANK

pre: pro:

pre:		pro:
pretender	....	PANJANDRUM
pretense	....	SIMULACRUM
pretty	....	INCONY
prevent	....	OBVIATE
preventative	....	PROPHYLACTIC
pride	....	HUBRIS
priently	....	HIERATIC
priestly	....	SACERDOTAL
primitive	....	TROGLODYTIC
proclaim	....	ASSEVERATE
proclaim	....	CONSUBSTANTIATE
proclaim	....	PROMULGE
proclaiming	....	INTERNUNCIAL
procrastinator	....	CUNCTATIVE
profane	....	RIBALD
profound	....	PROFUNDITY
projection	....	SCARCEMENT
prolific	....	UBEROUS
prone	....	COUCHANT
prone	....	RECUMBENT

pro: ## pus:

prophecy	....	AUGURY
prophetic	....	FATIDIC
prophetic	....	SIBYLLINE
prostitute	....	COURTESAN
prostitute	....	HETAERA
prostitute	....	QUEAN
prostitutes	....	DEMIMONDE
proud	....	ORGULOUS
proving	....	DEICTIC
proving	....	PROBATIVE
proximity	....	PROPINQUITY
pull-out	....	EDUCE
pun	....	EQUIVOQUE
pun	....	PARONOMASIA
punctual	....	PUNCTILIOUS
puncture	....	NYXIS
punish	....	FUSTIGATE
purging	....	LAPACTIC
purplish	....	HELIOTROPE
pussy	....	PURULENT

| put-in | .... | INTERCALATION |
| puzzling | .... | CRYPTIC |

chapter
q

qualm	....	COMPUNCTION
quarrelsome	....	FRACTIOUS
quarrelsome	....	PUGNACIOUS
quarrelsome	....	RUCTIOUS
quarrelsome	....	TRUCULENT
quarters	....	CANTONMENT
questions	....	INTERROGATORIES
quibble	....	CAVIL
quibble	....	PETTIFOG
quickening-music	....	ACCELERANDO
quotation	....	EPIGRAPH

chapter
r

racism	....	ETHNOCENTRICITY
rainy	....	PLUVIAN
rale	....	RHONCHUS
rambling	....	DISCURSIVE
random	....	ALEATORY
random	....	DESULTORY
random	....	STOCHASTIC
ranked	....	BREVETTED
rape	....	CONSTUPRATE
rapid-heart	....	TACHYCARDIA
rapture	....	NYMPHOLEPSY

ras: **red:**

rascal	....	SKELLUM
rash	....	IMPOLITIC
rationalist	....	CASUISTICAL
ravenous	....	ACORIA
ravenous	....	RAPACIOUS
ravishing	....	DEFLORATION
rearrange	....	ANAGRAM
reasoning	....	SYLLOGISM
rebel	....	INSURGENT
rebellious	....	ICONOCLAST
rebirth	....	PALINGENETIC
rebirth	....	RENAISSANCE
reception	....	LEVEE
reckless	....	TEMERARIOUS
recluse	....	ANCHORET
recluse	....	SOLITUDINARIAM
record	....	PROCESVERBAL
recurring	....	LEITMOTIF
reddish	....	RUFESCENT
reddish	....	RUFUS

red: ren:

reddish-orange	....	GRENADINE
redheaded	....	RUTILISM
reduction	....	DETUMESCENCE
redundancy	....	NIMIETY
reflecting	....	RELUCENT
regain	....	REPLEVY
regular	....	METRONOMIC
reject	....	IRRECUSABLE
relaxing	....	EMOLLIENT
release	....	REMIT
relentless	....	INEXORABLE
remember	....	ANAMNESIS
remorse	....	COMPUNCTION
removal	....	EXTIRPATION
remove	....	EXPURGATE
remove	....	ABLATE
remove	....	ABSCISSION
remove	....	RESECTION
renounce	....	ABJURE
renounce	....	FORSWEAR

ren: ## rev:

ren:		rev:
renovate	....	REDINTEGRATE
renunciation	....	ABNEGATION
repay	....	REPARATION
repeat	....	INGEMINATE
repeated	....	RECIDIVISM
repeating	....	ITERATION
repetitious	....	TAUTOLOGICAL
resentful	....	DUDGEON
reserved	....	DIFFIDENT
residue	....	RESIDUUM
resistant	....	RENITENT
respect	....	OBEISANT
responsive	....	ANTIPHONAL
restoration	....	APOCATASTASIS
restore	....	REVIVIFICATION
restore	....	REVIVIFY
return	....	RECRUDESCENCE
return	....	REPAIR
revel	....	ROISTER
revelation	....	DENOUEMENT

revile	....	VILIPEND
revision	....	RECENSION
revolution	....	JUNTO
revolution	....	LABEFACTION
revolve	....	CIRCUMVOLUTION
riddle	....	CONUNDRUM
right-handed	....	DEXTRAL
ring-shaped	....	ANNULAR
ringing	....	TINTINNABULATION
riotous	....	OCHLOCRATIC
rip	....	DISCERP
rising	....	ANABATIC
rising	....	ASSURGENT
robber	....	PICAROON
robber	....	YEGG
robe	....	VESTMENT
rod-like	....	BACULINE
roomy	....	CAPACIOUS
roomy	....	COMMODIOUS
rooting	....	RADICATE

rough	....	SCABROUS
roughness	....	ASPERITY
roundabout	....	PERIPHRASTIC
rubbing	....	EFFLEURAGE
rude	....	INSOLENT
ruffian	....	TATTERDEMALION
rural	....	CAMPESTRAL
rustic	....	BUCOLIC

chapter
s

sacrifice	....	IMMOLATE
sailing-ship	....	XEBEC
salary	....	EMOLUMENT
salivate	....	PTYALORRHEA
salivating	....	PITYALISM
same	....	IDENTIC
sandy	....	ARENOSE
sandy	....	SABULOUS
sarcastic	....	MORDANCY
sarcastic	....	SARDONIC
satire	....	PASQUINADE

satisfy	....	ASSUAGE
satisfy	....	SATIATE
saving	....	SALVIFIC
saying	....	APOETHM
saying	....	EPIGRAM
scale	....	ESCALADE
scholar	....	POLYHISTOR
scholarship	....	ERUDITION
school-of arts	....	CONSERVATORY
scoundrel	....	PICARESQUE
scoundrel	....	ROGUE
sea-battle	....	NAUMACHY
seam	....	RHAPHE
search	....	INDAGATE
sea-sickness	....	NAUPATHIA
seductive	....	FEMME FATALE
seize	....	RAVISH
self-arousal	....	AUTOEROTISM
self-assertive	....	BUMPTIOUS
self-denial	....	ASCETIC

sel: sep:

self-deprivation	....	MASOCHISM
self-educated	....	AUTODIDACT
self-gratification	....	INDULGENT
self-love	....	NARCISSISM
self-possessed	....	MEGALOMANIA
self-righteous	....	SENTENTIOUS
self-sufficient	....	INENARRABLE
self-taught	....	AUTODIDACTIC
self-written	....	HOLOGRAPHIC
senile	....	ANILE
senior	....	DOYEN
senior	....	SENECTITUDE
sensitive	....	SENSIFEROUS
sensual	....	VOLUPTUARY
sentimental	....	MAWKISH
sentimentality	....	BATHOS
separate	....	DISCRETE
separate	....	PRESCEND
separate	....	SEVERAL
separated	....	SEQUESTRATION

ser: shi:

series	....	POLYSTICHOUS
sermon	....	HOMILY
servitude	....	THRALDOM
sexual	....	APHRODISIAC
sexual	....	AMATORY
sexual	....	CONCUPISCENT
sexual	....	PRURIENT
sexuality	....	CONCUPISCENCE
shadowy	....	ADUMBRAL
shady	....	UMBRAGEOUS
shaking	....	JECTIGATION
shameful	....	INGLORIOUS
shameless	....	ARRANT
shapeless	....	AMORPHOUS
shaven	....	IMBERB
shavings	....	EXCELSIOR
sheathed	....	VAGINATE
sheltered	....	ENSCONCED
shield	....	ESCUTCHEON
shifty	....	LOUCHE

shoeless	....	DISCALCED
shore	....	LITTORAL
short-lived	....	EPHEMERAL
show-off	....	PEDANTIC
show-off	....	CYNOSURE
shrew	....	VIRAGO
shrew	....	XANTHIPPE
shy	....	CHARY
shy	....	NEBBISH
sickly	....	VALETUDINARIAN
sightless	....	TYPHLOSIS
silent	....	TACITURN
silver	....	ARGENT
sinful	....	PIACULAR
single	....	AGAMOUS
sinuous	....	ANFRACTUOUS
sisterly	....	SORORAL
sixtieth	....	SEXAGESIMAL
skepticism	....	NIHILISTIC
skillful	....	DAEDUL

sku: slu:

skull cap	....	ZUCCHETTO
skunk	....	CONEPATE
slander	....	ANIMADVERSION
slander	....	ASPERSION
slander	....	CALUMNY
slander	....	TRADUCE
slang	....	ARGOT
slavery	....	THRALL
slavish	....	OBSEQUIOUS
sleepiness	....	HYPNAGOGIC
sleepiness	....	SOPORIFIC
sleepwalker	....	NOCTAMBULIST
sleepwalking	....	SOMNAMBULISM
sleepy	....	SOMNOLENT
slender	....	ECTOMORPHIS
slight-of-hand	....	LEGERDEMAIN
slogan	....	SHIBBLETH
slow-heart	....	BRADYCARDIA
slug	....	LIMACINE
sluggish	....	TORPID

sluggishness	....	LANGUOR
small	....	LILLIPUTIAN
smell	....	OFACTION
smelling	....	OSMESIS
smelly	....	EFFLUVIUM
smoky	....	FULGINOUS
smooth	....	GLABROUS
smoothly	....	MELLIFLUOUS
smoothly	....	PROFLUENT
smug	....	PRIGGISH
snake	....	OPHIDIAN
sneeze	....	PTARMUS
snow-like	....	NIVEOUS
soak	....	MACERATE
socialism	....	ETATISM
society	....	SODALITY
sodomy	....	PEDERASTY
softening	....	RAMOLLISSEMENT
soiled	....	SCROFULOUS
solicit	....	IMPORTUNATE

somber	....	SOMBROUS
son-of-God	....	AVATAR
soothing	....	ABIRRITANT
soothing	....	DEMULCENT
sophisticated	....	SOIGNE
sound	....	SONANCE
sound-alike	....	ONOMATOPOEIA
sound-avoidance	....	PHONOPHOBIC
soupy	....	BISQUE
sour	....	ACESCENT
source	....	PROVENANCE
sparkle	....	CORUSATE
speaking	....	ELOCUTION
speculate	....	EXTRAPOLATE
speed	....	CELERITY
spherical	....	GLOBOUS
spicy	....	PIQUANT
spinning	....	STROBIC
spiral	....	HELICINE
spirit	....	ANIMUS

spirited	....	ELAN
sponge	....	MOREL
sponsorship	....	AEGIS
spotted	....	LENTIGINOUS
spotted	....	PIEBALD
spread	....	METASTASIZE
spreading	....	PROPOGATION
spreading	....	PROTUBERANT
spring	....	VERNAL
spring-back	....	RESILE
sprinkle	....	BESPANGLE
spruce-up	....	TIUITATE
stabbing	....	LANCINATING
staggering	....	TITUBATION
stalking	....	PREDACEOUS
standard	....	NORMATIVE
starchy	....	FARINALEOUS
starry	....	SIDEREAL
steady	....	EQUABLE
steal	....	FILCH

steal	....	SPOLIATE
stealthily	....	FURTIVELY
steep	....	PRECIPITOUS
steeple	....	FLECHE
sterility	....	AGENESIA
sterilize	....	ASEXUALIZATION
sterilize	....	AUTOCLAVE
stern	....	AUSTERE
stern	....	DOUR
stew	....	SLUMGULLION
sticky	....	VISCID
stimulation	....	ERETHISM
sting	....	TEREBRATE
stingy	....	PENURIOUS
stingy	....	ILLIBERAL
stinking	....	FETID
stinking	....	MALODOROUS
stolen	....	PURLOINED
stop	....	BELAY
stop	....	KIBOSH

storage	....	CACHE
story	....	ANECDOTAL
storyteller	....	RACONTEUR
straight	....	GEODESIC
strengthen	....	REBORANT
strip	....	DENUDE
stripper	....	EDCYSIAST
stroke	....	APOPLECTIC
strong	....	PUISSANT
stronghold	....	FASTNESS
stubborn	....	CAMSTAIRY
stubborn	....	MULISH
stubborn	....	RECALCITRANT
stuck-up	....	FROIDEUR
studio	....	ATELIER
study	....	LUCUBRATION
stupid	....	BOEOTIAN
stupid	....	DOLTISH
stupid	....	GORMLESS
stupid	....	MORONIC

stupor	....	PSYCHOCOMA
stern	....	DOUR
stutter	....	PSELLISM
style-of –writing	....	GENRE
submissive	....	UXORIOUS
subordinate	....	SUBALTERN
sucking	....	MYZESIS
suffocate	....	HYPOXIA
sugar	....	XYLOSE
suitable	....	BESEEM
suitable	....	IDONEOUS
suitcase	....	IMPEDIMENTA
suitcase	....	PORTMANTEAU
summary	....	COMPENDIUM
sun-centered	....	HELIOCENTRIC
sunstroke	....	HELIOSIS
superficial	....	DILATANTE
superficial	....	SCIOLISTIC
superfluous	....	SUPEREROGATORY
supernatural	....	PRETERNATURAL

sup: sym:

supplement	....	CODICIL
supplier	....	PURVEYOR
supporter	....	JANISSARY
supremely	....	SOVRANLY
surname	....	COGNOMEN
surname	....	PATRONYMIC
surplus	....	SURPLUSAGE
surrounding	....	AMBIENT
swagger	....	HECTOR
swallowing	....	DEGLUTITION
sweeper	....	BESOM
sweetheart	....	DOWSABEL
swelling	....	TUBER
swelling	....	TUMESENCE
swindler	....	GRIFTER
swishing	....	FROUFROU
swollen	....	TUMESCENT
symbol	....	EXPONENT
symbol	....	IDEOGRAM

chapter
t

tact	....	SAVOIR FAIRE
tactless	....	GUACHE
tailless	....	ANUROUS
tailored	....	SARTORIAL
talkative	....	EXPATIATING
talkative	....	GARRULITY
talkative	....	GARRULOUS
talkative	....	LOQUACIOUS
talkative	....	POPINJAY
tangent	....	ASYMPTOTE

tangible	....	TACTILE
tapering	....	LANCEOLATED
tasteful	....	PRECIOSITY
tasteless	....	INSIPID
teach	....	DIDACTIC
teaching	....	HEURISTIC
teaching	....	PEDAGOGY
tearful	....	LACHRYMOSE
tearing	....	AVULSION
tearing	....	LACRIMAL
teasing	....	BADINAGE
technical-terms	....	TERMINOLOGICAL
temperament	....	PANTAGRUELISM
temple-of-gods	....	PANTHEON
tenacious	....	PERTINACIOUS
tent	....	YURT
terminate	....	DISESTABLISH
terminate	....	SURCEASE
terrestrial	....	SUBLUNARY
thaw	....	EUTETIC

the: ## tim:

theatrical	....	DRAMATURGIC
theatrical	....	HISTRIONIC
theft	....	PRIGGERY
theory	....	HYPOTHESIS
thickened	....	INSPISSATED
thick-skinned	....	PACHYDERMATOUS
thin	....	GRACILE
thirdly	....	TERTIARY
thirst	....	ANADIPSIA
thirsty	....	POLYDIPSIA
threefold	....	TRIPLICITY
thrill	....	FRISSON
throng	....	UMBERMENT
throw	....	JACULATE
throwback	....	ATAVISM
throw-out	....	DEFENESTRATE
thrust-out	....	OBTRUDE
thrusting	....	ERUMPENT
timetable	....	SYNCHRONISM
timid	....	TIMOROUS

tin: **tre:**

tingling	....	PARESTHESIAS
tiny	....	DIMINUTIVE
tireless	....	INDEFATIGABLE
title	....	RUBRIC
toast	....	WASSAIL
tomboy	....	HOYDEN
tongue	....	LANGUET
toothache	....	ODONTALGIA
traitor	....	GUISLING
transcriber	....	AMANUENSIS
transfer	....	DEVOLUTION
transform	....	TRANSMOGRIFY
transform	....	TRANSMUTE
translation	....	RELEXIFICATION
transparent	....	DIAPHANOUS
transparent	....	PELLUCID
trap	....	ENTOIL
trees	....	BOSCAGE
tree-like	....	DENDROPHILOUS
trembling	....	TREMULOUS

triangular	....	SAGITATE
trick	....	ARTIFICE
trick	....	WAGGERY
trifle	....	BAGATELLE
trivial	....	DOGGERAL
troublemaker	....	FOMENTER
true	....	AXIOMATIC
trustworthy	....	MORIGERATE
truth	....	APHORISM
truth	....	VERISIMILITUDE
truthful	....	VERIDIC
tubular	....	CANNULAR
tumor	....	NAOPLASM
tuned-in	....	OBVOLUTE
turncoat	....	RECREANT
turreted	....	CASTELLATED
twilight	....	GLOAMING
two-edged	....	ANCIPITAL
typical	....	QUINTESSENTIAL

chapter
u

unauthorized	....	ULTRA VIRES
unbeliever	....	INFIDEL
unbiased	....	INDIFFERENT
uncertain	....	IDIOPATHIC
uncertainty	....	DUBIOSITY
unchangeable	....	IMMUTABLE
uncle-like	....	AVUNCULAR
unclear	....	AMPHIBOLOGY
unclear	....	AMPHIGORY
uncompromising	....	INTRANSIGENT

unc: ## uno:

unconsciousness	....	NARCOSIS
understanding	....	INTUITED
understanding	....	PERSPICACIOUS
understatement	....	LITOTES
understatement	....	MEIOSIS
uneducated	....	BOOBOISIE
unflappable	....	IMPERTURBATION
unfortunate	....	DISAMENITY
unfortunate	....	SCEVITY
unfriendly	....	INIMICAL
ungrammatical	....	SOLECISTIC
unilateral	....	SECUND
unintelligible	....	GLOSSOLALIA
unique	....	SINGULAR
unique	....	SUI GENERIS
united	....	SOLIDARY
unload	....	DISGORGE
unmixable	....	IMMISCIBLE
unnecessary	....	SUPERFLUOUS
unorthodox	....	HETERODOX

unprepared	....	IMPROVIDENT
unreasonable	....	CHAUVINISM
unremoved	....	UNEXPURGATED
unreturned	....	UNREQUITED
unruly	....	ACERBIC
unruly	....	OBSTREPEROUSNES
unruly	....	RESTIVE
unsaleable	....	INALIENABLE
unsatisfying	....	JEJUNE
unsolvable	....	IRREMEDIABLE
unspeakable	....	INEFFABLE
unstable	....	LABILE
unsteady	....	WAMBLE
unusual	....	DEUTEROPATHY
unusual	....	RECHERCHE
unusual	....	SELCOUTH
unwise	....	ANSERINE
uproot	....	DERACINATE
urbane	....	SVELTE
urbanization	....	CONURBATION

urg: ## uri:

urgency	....	EXIGENCY
urgent	....	NECESSITIOUS
urination	....	MICTURITION

chapter
v

vagrant	....	CLOCHARD
valor	....	VALIANCE
value	....	PETCOCK
vanish	....	EVANESCE
vengeance	....	COMMINATION
vent	....	FUMAROLE
ventilate	....	AERATE
ventilate	....	INSUFFLATE
verbose	....	BLOVIATE
verification	....	EMPIRICAL

ver: ## vul:

verification	....	EXISTENTIAL
vestibule	....	NARTHEX
vigorously	....	YERK
villain	....	MISCREANT
visions	....	PHANTASMOGORIA
volcanic	....	IGNEOUS
vomiting	....	HYPEREMESIS
vulgarity	....	BILLINGSGATE
vulture	....	AASVOGEL

chapter
w

wager	....	IMPONE
wail	....	ULULATE
wakefulness	....	PERVIGILIUM
walk	....	PEREGRINATE
wall	....	PARAPET
walled-over	....	IMMURED
wander	....	DIVAGATE
wander	....	GALLIVANT
wander	....	MAUNDER
wandering	....	VAGROM

wan:

wea:

want	....	APPETENCE
warning	....	CAVEAT
warning	....	PREMONITARY
warrant	....	CAPIAS
wart	....	EXCRESCENCE
wart	....	THYMION
wash	....	DETERGE
washing	....	ABLUTION
waste	....	DROSS
waste	....	OFFAL
waste	....	ORDURE
waterfall	....	SAULT
water-receptive	....	HYDROPHILIC
water-repellant	....	HYDROPHOBIC
weak	....	ACRASIA
weak	....	ASTHENIC
weak	....	THEWLESS
weaken	....	ATTENUATE
weaken	....	EMASCULATE
wealth	....	NABOBISM

wealthy	....	SYBARITE
weaning	....	ABLACTATION
weekly	....	HEBDOMEDAL
weird	....	ELDRITCH
well-dressed	....	CONCINNOUS
wetting	....	HUMECTANT
whim	....	CROTCHETY
whine	....	PULE
whip	....	FLAGELLATE
whirling	....	VERTIGINOUS
whirling	....	VORTIGINOUS
whirlpool	....	MAELSTROM
whispering	....	SUSURRATION
whispering	....	SUSURROUS
white	....	LEUKOUS
whiten	....	ETIOLATE
whitish	....	ALBESCENT
wicked	....	FACINOROUS
wicked	....	FLAGITIOUS
wickedness	....	INIQUITOUS

wid: wor:

widowhood   ....   VIDUITY

wig   ....   PERUKE

wildness   ....   FERITY

winding   ....   LABYRINTHIAN

winding   ....   SINUOUS

winegrower   ....   VIGNERON

wine-study   ....   OENOLOGY

wisdom   ....   SAGACITY

wisdom   ....   SAPIENCE

wish   ....   VELLEITY

wishful   ....   DESIDERATE

woman-hater   ....   MISOGAMY

womanhood   ....   MULIEBRITY

wood-carved   ....   BOISRERIE

wooded   ....   ABOREOUS

wooded   ....   BUSKY

wood-like   ....   LIGENOUS

wood-like   ....   XYLOID

word   ....   PALABRA

wordiness   ....   CIRCUMLOCUTION

wordiness	....	PERIPHRASIS
wordy	....	SESQUIPEDALIAN
wordy	....	PROLIX
worker	....	ROUSTABOUT
workmate	....	YOKEMATE
worried	....	SOLICITOUS
worsening	....	INGRAVESCENT
worthless	....	FECKLESS
wrinkled	....	RUGOSE
writer	....	PENSTER
writer	....	SCRIVENER

chapter
x

xed	....	DISESTABLISHED
x-ray	....	ROENTGEN

chapter
y

yahoo	....	PHILISTINE
yawn	....	OSCITANT
yawning	....	OSCITATION
yearly	....	ETESIAN
yearning	....	REPINE
yellow	....	XANTHIC
yielding	....	OBSEQUIOUS
yoke	....	YELK
youth	....	VIRIDITY
youth	....	NEOTERIC
youthful	....	JUVENESCENT

chapter
z

zap	....	INTERNECINE
zealot	....	DOCTRINAIRE
zealous	....	FERVID
zealous	....	PERFERID
zenith	....	ACME
zest	....	PIQUANCY
zip	....	VIM
zoned	....	CIRCUMSCRIBED

Printed in the United States
80980LV00001BA/4-42